MW01056957

BOOK
2

WORDLY WISE
3000®

Direct Academic Vocabulary Instruction

Fourth Edition

Kenneth Hodkinson • Sandra Adams • Erika Hodkinson

EDUCATORS PUBLISHING SERVICE
Cambridge and Toronto

Editorial team: Carolyn Daniels, Marie Sweetman, Erika Wentworth
Cover Design: Deborah Rodman, Karen Swyers
Interior Design: Deborah Rodman

Illustrations: Mike Dammer

©2018 by School Specialty, Inc. All rights reserved. No part of this book may be reproduced or utilized in any form or by any electronic or mechanical means, including photocopying, without permission in writing from the publisher.

Printed in Benton Harbor, MI, in May 2023
ISBN 978-0-8388-7705-0

6 7 8 PPG 25 24 23

Contents

Lesson 1 1
Bailey Finds a New Home   7

Lesson 1 Review   11

Lesson 2 12
Fast Food on the Fly   17

Lesson 2 Review   22

Lesson 3 23
Greetings from Mars   28

Lesson 3 Review   32

Lesson 4 33
Sa-so Says Hello   37

Lesson 4 Review   42

Lesson 5 43
The Talking Tree   49

Lesson 5 Review   53

Lesson 6 54
What It's Like to Be 300
Million Years Old   59

Lesson 6 Review   64

Lesson 7 65
Wave to Me, and I'll
Wave Back   71

Lesson 7 Review   75

Lesson 8 76
Get Close to Mother Nature   81

Review Lesson 8   85

Lesson 9 86
Going Around in Circles   92

Lesson 9 Review   96

Lesson 10 97
Twinkle, Twinkle, Little Star   102

Lesson 10 Review   107

Lesson 11 108
Watch Out for Dragons   113

Lesson 11 Review   117

Lesson 12 118
Castles of Sand   123

Lesson 12 Review   128

Lesson 13 129
The Lost City of the Incas   135

Lesson 13 Review   140

Lesson 14 141
Elephant Country   146

Lesson 14 Review   151

Lesson 15 152
Music of the Island   157

Lesson 15 Review   162

Welcome to *Wordly Wise 3000*®

You've been learning words since you were a tiny baby. At first, you learned them only by hearing other people talk. Now that you're a reader, you have another way to learn words.

When you read, it's important to know what *every* word means. You can try skipping a word you don't know. But this might cause a problem. Read this sentence:

Anyone without a megtab *will not get into the show.*

If you have no idea of what a *megtab* is, you might not get in. All of a sudden, knowing what that one word means is important!

The more words you know, the better. You will understand more of what you read. *Wordly Wise 3000* can't teach you *all* the words you'll need, but it will help you learn lots of them. It can also help you learn how to learn even more words.

How Do You Figure Out What a Word Means?

What should you do when you come to a word and you think you don't know what it means? Following some easy steps can help you.

Say It

First, sound it out. Then say it to yourself. It might sound like a word you know. Sometimes you know a word in your head without knowing what it looks like in print. So if you match up what you know and what you read—you have the word!

Use Context

If this doesn't work, take the next step: look at the context—the other words and sentences around it. Read this sentence:

When it rained, the dog looked for shelter *under the porch.*

If the word *shelter* doesn't look familiar, look at the words around it. *Rain* and *under the porch* might give you a clue. You might even do a Think-Aloud:

I know that if you don't want to get wet outside when it rains, you need to get under something. In this sentence, the dog went under the porch to stay dry. So shelter must mean "something that protects you." Yes, that makes sense in this sentence.

Use Word Parts

If the context doesn't help, look at the parts of the word. Does it have any parts you know? These can help you figure out what it means. Read this sentence:

The miners *put on their hard hats before going to work.*

If you don't know the meaning of *miner*, try looking at parts of the word. You might know that a *mine* is a place underground where people get coal and other valuable things. A lot of times, *-er* at the end of a word means "a person who does something." For example, a *teacher* teaches in a school. So a *miner* might be someone who works in a mine. You would put on a hard hat if you were going into a mine. That meaning of *miner* makes sense.

Look It Up

If saying the word or using context and word parts don't work, you can look it up. You can find the word in a dictionary—either a book or online—or a glossary.

Nobody knows the meaning of every word, but good readers know how to figure out words they don't know.

Study the words. Then do the exercises that follow.

calf

n. 1. The back part of the leg between the knee and the ankle.

My left **calf** itches where the poison ivy touched it.

2. A young cow or bull.

The baby **calf** stays close to its mother.

Show your partner the sound you think a calf might make.

claw

n. 1. The sharp curved nail on the toe of a bird or animal.

Karl held out his hand, and the parrot wrapped its **claws** around his finger.

2. The part of a crab or lobster used for gripping.

The lobster grabbed the clam with its big **claw** and held it.

v. To scratch or dig with sharp nails.

Our dog **clawed** at the back door so she could come into the house.

couple

n. 1. Two things of the same kind.

There are a **couple** of cups on the shelf. Will you bring me one?

2. Two people who do things together.

The **couple** skated slowly around the rink, moving with the music.

Point to a couple of things near you and tell your partner about them.

© SSI • DO NOT DUPLICATE

cushion

n. A pillow or a pad with a soft filling.

Tammy rested her head on the **cushion** and soon fell asleep.

 Tell your partner about a cushion you have at home.

flap

n. Something attached on only one side so that it can move freely.

Colin licked the **flap** of the envelope and then pressed it down.

v. To move up and down.

We heard the geese **flap** their wings as they flew over the pond.

 Show your partner how to act like a bird flapping its wings.

groom

n. 1. A person who takes care of horses.

The **groom** led the horse out of the stall to brush it.

2. A man who is getting married.

The **groom** slipped the wedding ring on the bride's finger.

v. To clean or make neat.

The mother cat **groomed** the kitten's fur by licking it until it was smooth.

share

n. A part that each person gets of a whole.
Your **share** of the pizza will be two slices.

v. To use or enjoy with others.
My sister and I **share** a bedroom.

Tell your partner about something you shared with a friend.

shelter

n. Anything that covers or protects.
Our dog looks for **shelter** under the bed when he hears thunder.

v. To give protection or safety to someone or something.
The small porch **sheltered** us from the rain.

yard

n. 1. The land around a building.
We lived in a house with a large **yard.**

2. A length equal to three feet, or thirty-six inches.
You need three **yards** of cloth to make your costume for the play.

zero

n. The word name for 0. It stands for nothing.
Three plus **zero** equals three.

© SSI • DO NOT DUPLICATE

1A Words and Their Meanings

1 to move up and down
(a) claw   (b) shelter   (c) flap   (d) groom

2 to use with others
(a) groom   (b) claw   (c) shelter   (d) share

3 the word name for 0
(a) couple   (b) zero   (c) yard   (d) calf

4 the land around a building
(a) yard   (b) groom   (c) claw   (d) cushion

5 something that protects
(a) calf   (b) shelter   (c) zero   (d) couple

Look at the word next to the number. Then circle the letter next to the group of words that has the same meaning.

calf
claw
couple
cushion
flap
groom
share
shelter
yard
zero

6 claw
(a) a person who takes care of horses   (b) the curved nail of a bird
(c) a length of three feet   (d) the curved horn of a cow

7 calf
(a) a baby sheep   (b) the arm between the hand and the elbow
(c) a baby horse   (d) the back of the leg between the knee and the ankle

8 couple

(a) a large number of things   (b) a man getting married

(c) two things of the same kind   (d) a woman getting married

9 groom

(a) to make clean and neat   (b) to use with others

(c) to move up and down   (d) to swing from side to side

10 cushion

(a) food for horses   (b) a pad with a soft filling

(c) a feeling of happiness   (d) a young cow

1B Seeing Connections

Look at each group of words. Three are related in some way. Find the one word that does not belong and circle it.

1	stool	wall	chair	cushion
2	seven	two	too	zero
3	pony	calf	elbow	knee
4	bride	groom	apple	ring
5	pair	two	couple	crowd

© SSI • DO NOT DUPLICATE

Applying Meanings

Circle the letter next to the correct answer.

1 Which of the following is equal to a **yard?**
(a) twelve inches (b) a couple (c) three feet (d) zero

2 Which of the following could provide **shelter?**
(a) a calf (b) a cushion (c) a claw (d) a cave

3 Which of the following has **claws?**
(a) a groom (b) a crab (c) a calf (d) a shark

4 Which of the following might have a **flap?**
(a) a tent (b) a couple (c) a bird (d) a swing

5 Which of the following cannot be **shared?**
(a) money (b) shelter (c) toys (d) zero

calf
claw
couple
cushion
flap
groom
share
shelter
yard
zero

Bailey Finds a New Home

Sandra Adams and Ken Hodkinson live at Sugar Wood Farm in New Hampshire. They have a cat named Bailey. He did not always live with them. If Bailey could talk, he might tell you how he came to live with Sandra and Ken. Let's imagine he can.

• • • • • • • • • • • •

At first, Ken and Sandra didn't want me. Many times I waited outside their door for them to return home. I knew I had only a **couple** of seconds to make my move. So I would rub against Sandra's **calf,** purring loudly and looking up at her face. But Ken always said, "Don't let him in. Don't let him in." And they shut the door in my face.

It's true that I already had a home. But I had to **share** it with two other cats who liked to bully me. That was no fun. I wanted something better. Sugar Wood Farm was just around the corner, and I checked it out carefully. I counted the cats that lived there. The number I came up with was **zero.** As we cats say, "Purr-fect!"

Weeks went by, and it was the same every time. I hung around the door for hours, and Ken and Sandra always closed it in my face. But I never gave up. Then, one dark and stormy night, my chance came. I was waiting for them to come home, as usual, when it started to rain. Now, cats know enough to get out of the rain. I could have taken **shelter** in their woodshed. But I wanted to be right there on the doorstep when they came home.

Before long, the rain turned to snow. This was even better. I was sure that no one would turn a cat away on such a night. I heard their car pull into the **yard.** Then I watched them hurry toward the house. As soon as they saw me, I started to meow like a little lost kitten.

© SSI • DO NOT DUPLICATE

In no time, I was inside the house. Sandra dried me with a warm, fluffy towel. Ken kept saying, "Don't feed him. Don't feed him." But I wasn't looking for food just then. I was looking for a new home. At last, I thought I had found it. I was right. Before long, they were feeding me. Sandra talked to my old owners about me. They missed me, but they had two other cats. I didn't feel bad.

Cats spend a lot of time sleeping, so Sandra made a soft **cushion** for me to use. To be honest, I prefer their bed. They also made a cat door for me with a little **flap.** I just push it open with my nose, and it closes behind me. Sandra likes to **groom** me. I think I do it better myself, but it gives her a lot of pleasure. I try not to sharpen my **claws** on their furniture. I think they are happy to have me around.

Answer each of the questions with a sentence.

. . . .

1 How did Bailey know there were **zero** cats at Sugar Wood Farm?

_____

_____

2 How do you know that Ken didn't want to **share** his home with Bailey?

_____

_____

3 Why do you think Bailey rubbed against Sandra's **calf** and not Ken's?

_____

_____

4 Why didn't Bailey look for **shelter** when it started to rain and then snow?

_____

_____

calf
claw
couple
cushion
flap
groom
share
shelter
yard
zero

5 What happened to Bailey a **couple** of days after he was let into the house?

_____

_____

6 How do you know that Bailey can come in and go out to the **yard** easily?

_____

_____

7 Why didn't Bailey need to have Sandra **groom** him?

_____

_____

8 How often do you think Bailey sleeps on the **cushion** Sandra made for him? Explain your answer.

_____

_____

9 Do you think Bailey likes having the cat door with the **flap?** Explain your answer.

_____

_____

10 What are some ways Bailey might use his **claws?**

_____

_____

Fun FACT

- The plural of **calf** is not **calfs,** as you might expect. The plural of **calf** is **calves.**

© SSI • DO NOT DUPLICATE

1 **V**ocabulary **E**xtension

share

verb To use or enjoy with others.

noun A part that each person gets of a whole.

· ·

Academic Context

In school, **sharing** is telling others something. You can **share** stories or ideas or read something aloud that you wrote.

Discussion & Writing Prompt

Tell about a time you or someone else **shared** a story in class.

2 min.	3 min.
1. Turn and talk to your partner or group.	**2.** Write 1–3 sentences.
Use this space to take notes or draw your ideas.	Be ready to share what you have written.

Lesson 1

Review

© SSI • DO NOT DUPLICATE

Hidden Message Write the word that is missing from each sentence in the boxes next to it. The number after each sentence is the lesson the word is from. The shaded boxes will answer this riddle:

Joanne bet Joe that her dog could jump higher than a house. How did she win the bet?

1. The cloth was one _____ wide. (1)

2. Sue forgot her lunch, so I offered to _____ mine with her. (1)

3. _____ is the opposite of bad.

4. Ramon needs a _____ of stamps for his letter. (1)

5. Ellen put the _____ back on the sofa, after it fell. (1)

6. Three, two, one, _____ (1)

7. The kitten scratched my arm with its _____. (1)

8. The baby _____ followed its mother to the barn. (1)

9. The children ran for _____ as soon as the rain started. (1)

N'

10. The opposite of in is _____.

11. The _____ leads the horse to the stable. (1)

12. Large birds must _____ their wings to get into the air. (1)

J

Study the words. Then do the exercises that follow.

accident

n. Anything that happens in an unplanned way, especially when it causes injury or damage.

The **accident** happened when one car went through a red light and hit another one.

acrobat

n. A person who does tricks that take great strength and good control in moving the body.

The **acrobat** did a flip on the tightrope, and the crowd in the circus tent gasped.

alarm

n. 1. A signal, such as a bell or buzzer, that warns people or tells them to take action.

Beth shut off the **alarm** on the clock and went back to sleep.

2. A feeling that something is wrong or that there is danger.

Pete was filled with **alarm** when he lost his way in the woods.

v. To make somebody afraid or fearful.

I don't want to **alarm** you, but what is that noise in the backyard?

 Tell your partner about an alarm you have heard.

bounce

v. To spring back after hitting something.

The ball **bounced** three feet in the air after Maya hit it with her racket.

enormous

adj. Very big.

An elephant must seem **enormous** to a mouse.

Show your partner how to act like you are carrying something enormous.

gap

n. An opening or space in something that is normally closed.

The rabbit got into the garden through a **gap** in the fence.

Show your partner a gap using your hands.

scoop

n. A tool like a bowl with a handle. It can be large or small and is used for digging into and lifting loose or soft materials.

Mother used a metal **scoop** to put flour into the mixing bowl.

v. To take something up in a quick movement.

Dan cupped his hands to **scoop** water from the pond.

support

n. Something used to hold an object in place and to keep it from falling.

The shelf will fall without the wooden **support.**

v. To hold something in place or to keep it from falling.

Anne **supported** the sign while Ryan nailed it to the post.

Tell your partner how chairs support people.

© SSI • DO NOT DUPLICATE

tangle

    n. A mix-up of things twisted or knotted together.

    The fishing line was in such a **tangle** that Bill had to cut it.

    v. To become twisted or knotted together.

    I tripped and fell when my feet got **tangled** in the rope.

weigh

    v. To find out how heavy something is.

    Lucy **weighed** the puppy and learned that it had gained almost two pounds since last week.

    weight *n.* The measure of how heavy something is.

    The **weight** of a stick of butter is four ounces.

 Tell your partner about something that weighs a lot.

2A Completing Sentences

Circle each answer choice that correctly completes the sentence. Each question has three correct answers.

1 The **accident**

    (a) would not have happened if you had been careful.

    (b) was taken to the nearest hospital.

    (c) happened when I hit the tree with my bike.

    (d) was caused by the driver talking on his cell phone.

② The **tangle**

(a) of hooks and fishing lines had been left in a pile on the floor.

(b) in my foot was so bad that I had to scratch it.

(c) of knots in my sister's hair was impossible to brush.

(d) of bed sheets had somehow wrapped itself around me.

③ It **alarmed** me

(a) when no one answered the phone.

(b) when the caller refused to give her name.

(c) of certain facts that I had not known about.

(d) that no one seemed worried about the coming storm.

④ The **gap**

(a) we had to climb was over two hundred feet high.

(b) in the fence had been covered with a piece of wood.

(c) in the diary ran from June to July.

(d) was wide enough for me to peek through.

⑤ We know that the **weight**

(a) of the rock is over two tons.

(b) of the feather is almost nothing.

(c) can be measured in pounds.

(d) will be over an hour, but we still have to stay.

2B

Making Connections

Circle the letter next to the correct answer.

① Which word goes with *ball?*

(a) accident   (b) bounce   (c) support   (d) alarm

② Which word goes with *circus?*

(a) tangle   (b) gap   (c) scoop   (d) acrobat

© SSI • DO NOT DUPLICATE

3 Which word goes with *ice cream?*

(a) scoop   (b) yard   (c) flap   (d) weigh

4 Which word goes with *whale?*

(a) claw   (b) shelter   (c) enormous   (d) support

5 Which word goes with *carry?*

(a) support   (b) share   (c) alarm   (d) tangle

2C   Using Context Clues

Circle the letter next to the word that correctly completes the sentence.

1 The _____ hat didn't fit my small head.

(a) supported   (b) tangled   (c) enormous   (d) groomed

2 A stack of bricks can be used as a(n) _____.

(a) support   (b) scoop   (c) cushion   (d) alarm

3 A(n) _____ belongs at a circus.

(a) acrobat   (b) groom   (c) calf   (d) accident

4 Please do not _____ the ball against the window.

(a) tangle   (b) repair   (c) bounce   (d) support

5 Aisha _____ the tomatoes to see how heavy they were.

(a) bounced   (b) scooped   (c) supported   (d) weighed

accident
acrobat
alarm
bounce
enormous
gap
scoop
support
tangle
weigh

Fast Food on the Fly

Have you ever seen a bat hanging in some high corner of a room? Were you afraid? A bat can't talk. But imagine it could. Let's hear what it has to say.

• • • • • • • • • • • •

You probably think I'm ugly. A lot of people do. Maybe it's my wide wings, **enormous** ears, and small body. Some people are afraid of bats because they think we will get **tangled** in their hair. That's silly. I can fly through a **gap** in a fence no wider than your hand, and I don't even touch the sides with my wings. Do you think I'm going to fly by **accident** into someone's hair? It's not very likely.

Here is another thing you should know. I'm nosy, just like people. If I see a small opening near the roof or in the wall, I like to find out what's on the other side. So if you see me fly into your house, just open some doors and windows to help me get out. I don't want to be there any more than you want me there.

I am a small brown bat. I **weigh** less than half an ounce. Because I am so light, I fly very well. I'm like an **acrobat** in the air. I need to be. My food is flying insects. Once I spot one, I go after it and **scoop** it up in my mouth. And I do it in the dark. Pretty clever, don't you think? People hate mosquitoes because they bite. But we bats love them. It is easy for me to eat a couple of hundred bugs and still be hungry for more.

You probably don't believe that I can catch bugs in the dark. But it's true! That's because I "see" them with my ears.

© SSI • DO NOT DUPLICATE

Here's how I do it. I make sounds that are so high you can't even hear them. No human can. These sounds hit the bug I'm chasing. Then they **bounce** back to me. The sounds tell me just where the bug is as I fly after it. My big ears help me catch the sounds. No matter how much it tries to get away, the bug doesn't have a chance.

Did you know that bats sleep by hanging upside down? This may seem strange, but there is a good reason for it. When I want to fly, all I have to do is let go and I'm in the air. I'm flying! If I started from the ground, my legs could not **support** me. All bats are like that. We have very strong wings but weak legs.

So when you see a bunch of us swooping and flying in circles just as it's getting dark, don't be **alarmed.** That's when the bugs come out. Flying bugs are our fast food. That is, they are fast, but we are faster. We are just enjoying our dinner.

Answer each of the questions with a sentence.

1 How do you know that a bat **weighs** more than a mosquito?

_____

_____

2 Which part of its body does a bat use to **scoop** up mosquitoes?

_____

_____

3 Why isn't a bat **alarmed** if it suddenly falls while sleeping?

_____

_____

4 How are a bat and an **acrobat** alike?

_____

_____

accident
acrobat
alarm
bounce
enormous
gap
scoop
support
tangle
weigh

5 Which **supports** a bat better, its wings or its legs? Why?

_____

_____

6 Do bats fly into houses by **accident?** Explain your answer.

_____

_____

7 How do bats and people feel about **enormous** numbers of mosquitoes in the air?

_____

_____

8 Why would you look for small holes or **gaps** if a bat got into your house?

_____

_____

9 What are some things the sounds of a bat **bounce** back from?

_____

_____

10 Why is it unlikely that a bat will become **tangled** in a tree even if it is dark?

_____

_____

© SSI • DO NOT DUPLICATE

Fun FACT

- **Weigh** and **way** sound the same but mean different things. So do **weight** and **wait.** Words that sound the same but mean different things are called homophones.

support

verb To hold something in place or to keep it from falling.

noun Something used to hold an object in place and to keep it from falling.

Other Meanings

To **support** someone is to help or be kind to that person.
To **support** an idea is to agree with the idea or give reasons why you think it is true.

Word Family

un**support**ed (adjective)

supporting (adjective)

supportive (adjective)

Discussion & Writing Prompt

*My grandma is very **supportive**. When I am sad, she hugs me and tells me she loves me.*

After reading these sentences, what do you think **supportive** means?

2 min.	3 min.
1. Turn and talk to your partner or group.	2. Write 1–3 sentences.
Use this space to take notes or draw your ideas.	Be ready to share what you have written.

© SSI • DO NOT DUPLICATE

Review

Crossword Puzzle Solve the puzzle by writing the missing word in each sentence in the boxes with the matching numbers. The number after each clue is the lesson the word is from.

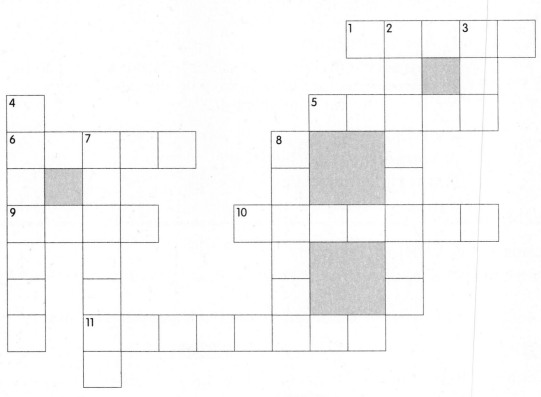

ACROSS

1. How many pounds do you_____? (2)

5. Hector used this metal _____ to serve ice cream. (2)

6. When the children heard the fire _____, they left the building. (2)

9. The opposite of boy is _____.

10. This piece of wood will _____ the table until we can fix the leg. (2)

11. Rosa threw the ball through the window by _____. (2)

DOWN

2. The size of this airplane is _____. (2)

3. The fence has a big _____ where the tree fell on it. (2)

4. The tail on Jaime's kite got _____ in the tree. (2)

7. We clapped when the _____ did a back flip. (2)

8. Please _____ the ball and throw it to the next player. (2)

Study the words. Then do the exercises that follow.

antenna

n. 1. One of the two long, thin feelers on the head of many insects and of some animals such as lobsters.

The beetle moved one **antenna** to the left when Sam touched it.

2. A metal rod or wire used to send and receive radio and television messages.

Let's pull out the **antenna** on the radio to hear the station more clearly.

balance

n. The state of being firm and steady.

Tanya lost her **balance** on the diving board and fell into the pool.

v. 1. To stay in a steady position without falling.

The acrobat **balanced** carefully on her partner's shoulders.

2. To hold something in a steady position without letting it fall.

The seal **balanced** a large ball on its nose.

• •

Show your partner how long you can balance on one foot.

boulder

n. A large, rounded rock that is resting on or in the ground.

On our hike, we followed the trail past a **boulder** as big as a car.

© SSI • DO NOT DUPLICATE

cliff

n. A steep, high rock face with a sharp drop to the ground below.

From the top of the **cliff,** the hunters watched the buffalo far below.

joint

n. The place where two parts meet or come together.

The elbow is the **joint** where the upper arm and lower arm connect.

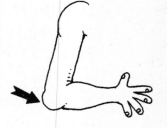

 Point to a joint in your body with your partner.

machine

n. An object with moving parts that is used to do certain kinds of work.

After we waxed the floor by hand, Jerome used a **machine** to polish it.

motor

n. An object that provides the power to make something move or do work.

Dad started the **motor** on the boat by pulling on the cord.

 Tell your partner about something that has a motor.

muscle

n. A part of the body that can be stretched or tightened to make the body move.

The day after we ran around the track, my leg **muscles** were sore.

 Show your partner where you have a muscle in your arm.

planet

n. A large object in space that moves in a regular path around the sun or some other star.

The rings around the **planet** Saturn are made up of many pieces of ice.

slope

n. A surface, a line, or a piece of land that is higher at one point than at another.

This ski **slope** is too steep for beginners.

v. To lie at an angle.

The land **slopes** up a little here by the pond.

Tell your partner about a time you ran or slid down a slope.

3A Words and Their Meanings

Look at the group of words next to the number. Then circle the letter next to the word that has the same meaning.

1 a part of the body that we can stretch or tighten

   (a) antenna   (b) motor   (c) muscle   (d) balance

2 an object that does work

   (a) machine   (b) boulder   (c) cliff   (d) planet

3 a long thin feeler on an insect

   (a) slope   (b) joint   (c) motor   (d) antenna

© SSI • DO NOT DUPLICATE

4 a state of being steady

(a) boulder   (b) balance   (c) planet   (d) joint

5 an object that provides the power to move something

(a) cliff   (b) motor   (c) boulder   (d) slope

Look at the word next to the number. Then circle the letter next to the group of words that has the same meaning.

6 cliff

(a) the sharp nail of a bird

(b) a metal rod used to receive messages

(c) a steep, high rock face

(d) an open space

7 planet

(a) a small airplane

(b) a large object that circles the sun

(c) a flat surface

(d) a door that swings freely

8 slope

(a) to scratch or dig

(b) to spring back after hitting something

(c) to stay in a steady position

(d) to lie at an angle

9 joint

(a) the place where two parts meet

(b) a glue to hold parts together

(c) the place where two streets meet

(d) an object that does work

10 boulder

(a) a loose article of clothing

(b) a part of the body

(c) a large rock

(d) a tool like a bowl with a handle

antenna
balance
boulder
cliff
joint
machine
motor
muscle
planet
slope

3B

Seeing Connections

Look at each group of words. Three are related in some way. Find the one word that does not belong and circle it.

1. stone   bridge   boulder   rock

2. antenna   eyes   claw   motor

3. skin   wood   muscle   bone

4. star   moon   joint   planet

5. balanced   steady   even   afraid

3C

Applying Meanings

Circle the letter next to the correct answer.

1. Which of the following can **slope?**
   (a) a yard   (b) a song   (c) a taste   (d) a smell

2. Which of the following is a **joint?**
   (a) a gap   (b) a knee   (c) a ball   (d) a muscle

3. Which of the following is not a **machine?**
   (a) toaster   (b) car   (c) computer   (d) nail

4. Which of the following describes a **cliff?**
   (a) loud   (b) happy   (c) high   (d) sweet

5. Which of the following has an **antenna?**
   (a) a lobster   (b) an elephant   (c) a rabbit   (d) a plant

© SSI • DO NOT DUPLICATE

3D Vocabulary in Context
Read the passage.

Greetings from Mars

You have probably seen pictures of robots. Imagine that a robot could talk to you about itself. It might say something like this.

• • • • • • • • • • • •

Hello, my name is Curiosity. I didn't grow from a seed or an egg, as plants and animals do. People made me to explore Mars. Mars is a **planet** that humans hope to visit one day. That's where I am now. I set off from Earth in 2012.

You and I do many of the same things, but we do them in different ways. When you move around or pick things up, you use your **muscles.** The power they have comes from the food you eat. Each move I make is caused by a little **motor.** I have many inside me. Their power comes from electricity. My computer controls all of them.

I don't have eyes. In their place I have television cameras. They send pictures to my computer. I can look to the right or left, up or down, wherever the computer tells me to. If I am exploring a place with many **boulders,** my television cameras tell my computer. Then it helps me go around them. If I get too close to a **cliff,** my computer again helps me move out of danger. I don't have ears either. Instead my **antenna** picks up messages sent by humans back in the United States. It also sends messages back to them.

I do all kinds of work. Some jobs I do better than humans. This is because I never get tired. As long as I have electricity, I keep on working. I can also work in places where it is difficult for people to go. On Mars, there is no air and very little water. Humans need both. I get along just fine without them.

Some robots stay in one place. I move around on six wheels. If I find myself going down a **slope,** my computer keeps me from falling over. If that were to happen, I wouldn't be able to get back on my wheels again. Just like people, I

| antenna |
| balance |
| boulder |
| cliff |
| joint |
| machine |
| motor |
| muscle |
| planet |
| slope |

have to keep my **balance.** I don't want to have an accident while I'm moving about.

You have two arms. I have only one. It has **joints** in it, like your wrist and elbow, but my arm is made of metal. It has a scoop at the end of it that I can use to dig into the ground. Everything I learn goes into my computer. Humans built me to find out what it is like here on Mars. They will use what they learned when the first humans come here.

I will never return home to Earth. How do I feel about that? Well, I don't have feelings. I'm never sad, but I'm also never happy. That's because I'm a **machine.** So staying here on Mars doesn't bother me at all.

Answer each of the questions with a sentence.

1 What happens to the **motor** of a robot if the electricity is shut off?

_____

_____

2 How do you know that Curiosity will probably not fall off a **cliff?**

_____

_____

3 What might happen to Curiosity if its **antenna** breaks off?

_____

_____

4 What would happen if Curiosity did not have **joints** in its arm?

_____

_____

5 How does Curiosity know when a **boulder** is in its path?

_____

_____

© SSI • DO NOT DUPLICATE

6 Why do robots never have sore **muscles?**

_____

_____

7 What might happen if Curiosity fell down a **slope?**

_____

_____

8 What helps Curiosity to keep its **balance?**

_____

_____

9 What are some important differences between **machines** and humans?

_____

_____

10 Would you like to visit another **planet** someday? Explain your answer.

_____

_____

| antenna |
| balance |
| boulder |
| cliff |
| joint |
| machine |
| motor |
| muscle |
| planet |
| slope |

Fun FACT

• Do you know the difference between **muscle** and **mussel?** These two words are pronounced the same but have different spellings and meanings. A **mussel** is a kind of shellfish with a long, slender, dark blue shell.

balance

noun The state of being firm and steady.

verb To stay in a steady position without falling.

Academic Context

To see if two things weigh the same, you can **balance** them on a scale. If one thing is heavier than the other, it will make that side of the scale go down.

Word Family

balanced (adjective)

balancing (adjective)

im**balance** (noun)

Discussion & Writing Prompt

What would happen if you put a big rock on one side of a scale and a feather on the other?

2 min.	**3 min.**
1. Turn and talk to your partner or group.	**2.** Write 1–3 sentences.
Use this space to take notes or draw your ideas.	Be ready to share what you have written.

© SSI • DO NOT DUPLICATE

Review

Hidden Message Write the word that is missing from each sentence in the boxes next to it. All the words are from Lesson 3. The shaded boxes will answer this riddle:

You throw away the outside and cook the inside; then you eat the outside and throw away the inside. What is it?

1. Gita lost her _____ and fell off the stone wall.

2. The _____ in the robot's leg needs to be oiled.

3. My arm _____ hurts from throwing the ball.

4. The _____ Mars has little water.

5. This large _____ fell from higher up the mountain.

6. The lighthouse stood on top of the _____.

7. The post office uses this _____ to stamp the letters.

8. This _____ is the best place to skateboard.

9. You can't hear the electric _____ on this fan.

10. Curiosity's _____ helps it send messages from Mars to Earth.

Study the words. Then do the exercises that follow.

ape

n. A large, strong animal related to monkeys but without a tail. It can stand on two feet.

Gorillas and chimpanzees are members of the **ape** family.

v. To copy the actions or speech of someone.

Trying to **ape** the chicken's walk made Millie look silly.

brain

n. The gray matter made of nerve cells packed inside the skull. It is what we think with. It controls other parts of the body.

If I use my **brain,** I think I can find an answer to this problem.

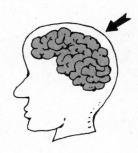

Talk to your partner about what living things have a brain.

branch

n. 1. A part of a tree that grows out of its main stem.

Mom and Dad hung the swing from a thick **branch** of the beech tree.

2. Anything that comes from a main part of something, as a branch comes from a tree.

Donna goes to the **branch** of the library near her home because the main library is too far away.

Show your partner how each of your fingers is a branch of your hand.

© SSI • DO NOT DUPLICATE

cavern

n. A large cave.

The roof of the **cavern** was covered with bats.

chimney

n. Something made with an open center to let the smoke from a fire rise and escape outside.

As we skied past the cabin, we saw smoke coming from the **chimney.**

dozen

n. A group of twelve.

Manuel invited a **dozen** friends to his party.

 Jump up and down a dozen times with your partner.

flame

n. The bright, glowing gas we see when something burns.

Three moths flew around the candle **flame.**

 Plan with your partner what you would do if you saw flames.

net

n. A piece of material made of string or rope knotted together in a way that leaves evenly spaced holes.

The fishermen repaired some torn parts of their **net.**

 Talk to your partner about something you might catch in a net.

spear

> *n.* A long pole with a sharp, pointed blade at one end.
>
> In the museum, we saw several **spears** used long ago to hunt animals.

torch

> *n.* A burning stick held in the hand to give light.
>
> The runner carried the Olympic **torch** to the city where the games were going to begin.

4A Completing Sentences

Circle each answer choice that correctly completes the sentence. Each question has three correct answers.

1 The **ape**

(a) is an animal that lives in the rain forest.

(b) at the zoo was the first born to the two gorillas.

(c) does not use a tail for balance, unlike a monkey.

(d) has a long trunk that it uses to drink water.

2 The **net**

(a) held less than a gallon of water.

(b) allowed smaller fish to escape.

(c) was pulled behind the boat.

(d) was left on the rocks to dry in the sun.

3 The **torch**

(a) stayed lit for over an hour.

(b) we carried into the cavern made spooky shadows.

(c) was made of branches twisted together.

(d) was written in black ink on pink paper.

© SSI • DO NOT DUPLICATE

4 The **flame** from the candle

(a) set the curtains on fire and caused the accident.

(b) gave enough light to read by.

(c) weighed a couple of pounds.

(d) was blown out by a gust of wind.

5 The **brain** of a human

(a) is larger than a mouse's.

(b) is made of plastic.

(c) can be protected by wearing a helmet.

(d) is where we do our thinking.

4B Making Connections

Circle the letter next to the correct answer.

1 Which word goes with *cave?*

(a) chimney   (b) cavern   (c) motor   (d) brain

2 Which word goes with *sharp?*

(a) zero   (b) net   (c) spear   (d) couple

3 Which word goes with *twelve?*

(a) dozen   (b) swamp   (c) chimney   (d) joint

4 Which word goes with *smoke?*

(a) boulder   (b) net   (c) brain   (d) chimney

5 Which word goes with *tree?*

(a) flap   (b) branch   (c) claw   (d) net

ape
brain
branch
cavern
chimney
dozen
flame
net
spear
torch

4C

Using Context Clues

Circle the letter next to the word that correctly completes the sentence.

1 Light the _____ and hold it up so we can see in the dark.
(a) cushion   (b) motor   (c) torch   (d) spear

2 It's rude to _____ your friend's limp.
(a) ape   (b) weigh   (c) balance   (d) slope

3 Throw the _____ at the target.
(a) cliff   (b) acrobat   (c) cavern   (d) spear

4 The main library has a couple of smaller _____.
(a) caverns   (b) branches   (c) spears   (d) torches

5 Use the _____ to catch the crab.
(a) net   (b) torch   (c) shelter   (d) boulder

4D

Vocabulary in Context

Read the passage.

Sa-so Says Hello

What do you think life was like long, long ago? What if you could travel back in time thousands of years? What if you could meet someone your own age from back then? Imagine what that person might say to you.

• • • • • • • • • • •

Hello! My name is Sa-so. I live in a time that you call the Ice Age. That is because ice covers much of the land. But not the part where I live. My family and I and some other families live in a **cavern.** We enter through a small opening. Inside there is a lot of room. We always have a fire burning. This

© SSi · DO NOT DUPLICATE

keeps us warm and dry. At night, the **flames** give us light to see by. Our large cave has a hole in the ceiling. It acts as a **chimney.** This keeps our shelter cozy.

You might think that because we live in a cave we're not much different from **apes.** But that's not true. I look like you. My **brain** is about the same size as yours, too. Of course, my life is different from yours in many ways. You live in a house or apartment. And you wear clothes that are cut to fit your body. My clothes are made from animal skins. I wrap them around me to keep warm.

You probably own lots of things. I have very few. First, I have my furs. They cover me and keep me warm at night. Second, I have some sharp stones. I use these as tools to cut and make things. Third, I have a necklace of shells. My mother made it for me. Last, I have my **spear.** I practice throwing it every day. My arm is becoming stronger. My aim is becoming more exact. I'm too young to go with the hunters now. But one day I'll join them to hunt large animals like deer, wild horses, and tigers. For now, I use a **net** to catch fish, birds, and small animals.

In my family, I'm the youngest. My job is to keep our fire burning while the others are busy. Some are out hunting. Others are looking for berries and other things to eat. When the fire starts to get low, I add some dry **branches** to it. It is very bad for us if the fire goes out. The only way we can get a new fire is to wait for one to start in the forest from lightning. Then we go there to light a **torch** and carry the fire back to our cave. But until then, we have to live in the cold and the dark. Even our food is cold. I don't want this to happen. So I am always careful to keep the fire burning.

We live near the front of our cave. But deep inside there are many large spaces. The walls are covered with **dozens** of pictures of animals that we hunt. We draw these pictures to bring the hunters good luck. Perhaps these paintings will still be there thousands of years from now. Then you and other people can visit our cave and see them for yourself.

ape
brain
branch
cavern
chimney
dozen
flame
net
spear
torch

Answer each of the questions with a sentence.

. . . .

❶ What are some things Sa-so can do that **apes** cannot do?

_____

_____

❷ Why do you think Sa-so will make sure he has a lot of **branches** near the fire?

_____

_____

❸ What are some animals Sa-so will probably hunt with his **spear** when he is older?

_____

_____

❹ How do you know that a **dozen** people could live in Sa-so's cave?

_____

_____

❺ For what reasons would Sa-so and his family use a **torch?**

_____

_____

❻ How might Sa-so use a **net** to catch small animals?

_____

_____

❼ What is one example from the passage of Sa-so using his **brain?**

_____

_____

© SSI • DO NOT DUPLICATE

8 What will happen if Sa-so lets the **flames** of the fire go out?

_____

_____

9 What are some things that make a **cavern** a good shelter for Sa-so and his family?

_____

_____

10 Why is it important to have a hole in the ceiling of the cave to act as a **chimney?**

_____

_____

Fun
FACT
• •
• In England, a flashlight is called a **torch.**

| ape |
| brain |
| branch |
| cavern |
| chimney |
| dozen |
| flame |
| net |
| spear |
| torch |

Vocabulary Extension

branch

noun A part of a tree that grows out of its trunk.

noun Anything that comes from a main part of something.

. . . .

Phrasal Verbs

branch off To come out from the main part of something and go in a different direction—just like the **branch** on a tree.

*The small streams **branch off** from the main river.*

Discussion & Writing Prompt

A big road can have smaller streets **branching off** from it. Can you think of something else big that has small things **branching off** from it?

2 min.	3 min.
1. Turn and talk to your partner or group.	**2.** Write 1–3 sentences.
Use this space to take notes or draw your ideas.	Be ready to share what you have written.
	_____
	_____
	_____
	_____
	_____
	_____
	_____
	_____
	_____
	_____
	_____

© SSI • DO NOT DUPLICATE

Review

Crossword Puzzle Solve the puzzle by writing the missing word in each sentence in the boxes with the matching numbers. The number after each clue is the lesson the word is from.

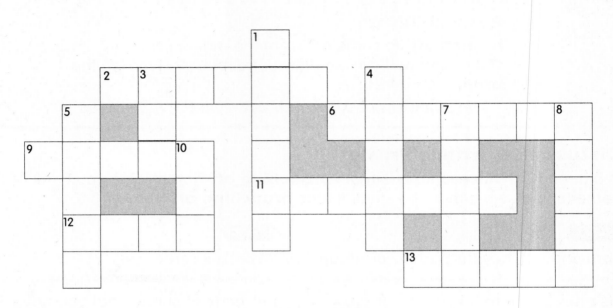

ACROSS

2. We saw some bats flying out of the _____. (4)

6. Tina wears _____ when she reads.

9. We picked a _____ ears of corn for the picnic. (4)

11. Look at all the smoke coming from that _____. (4)

12. How much does a pair of ice skates _____?

13. You use your _____ to think. (4)

DOWN

1. During the storm, a big _____ fell from the maple tree. (4)

3. At the zoo, we saw an _____ with its baby. (4)

4. The _____ of one candle does not give much light in this large room. (4)

5. A runner carried the _____ into the Olympic stadium. (4)

7. This _____ was used long ago to hunt animals. (4)

8. Four plus three minus zero equals _____.

10. Nico kicked the ball into the _____ and scored a point. (4)

Study the words. Then do the exercises that follow.

absorb

v. To take in or soak up.

This sponge will **absorb** the water you spilled.

 Tell your partner about something you spilled that had to be absorbed by a towel.

anchor

n. A heavy weight on a rope or chain. It is dropped from a boat to keep it from moving.

As our boat came near the shore, we dropped the **anchor** for the night.

v. To hold something firmly in place.

We need longer screws to **anchor** the cabinet to the wall.

 Show your partner how you would look if your feet were anchored to the floor.

brush

n. An object made of short, stiff hairs or wires that are fastened to a handle.

This wire **brush** works very well to scrape the old paint from the side of the house.

v. 1. To clean, paint, or smooth something by using a brush.

Leah **brushes** her teeth every night before going to bed.

2. To touch something lightly by moving against it.

Alex jumped when something **brushed** against his cheek in the dark hallway.

© SSI • DO NOT DUPLICATE

bud

n. A small swelling on a plant that will grow into a twig, flower, or leaf.

Aunt Jane told me to pick the roses that were open and to leave the **buds** on the bush.

center

n. 1. The exact middle of something.

The referee put the soccer ball in the **center** of the field just before the game started.

2. A place where people come together for some purpose.

Sara went with her mother to the health **center** for a checkup.

 Tell your partner where you think the center of the classroom is.

core

n. The hard middle part of fruits such as apples or pears. It holds the seeds of the plant.

Juan ate the apple and then gave the **core** to his pony.

 Tell your partner what you do with the core after you eat an apple.

factory

n. A building or group of buildings where things are made.

Natalie's sister works in a **factory** that makes parts for computers.

hive

n. The place where bees live.

Mr. Olach keeps several **hives** in his backyard for bees.

sapling

n. A young tree.

In this old photograph, you can see our great oak tree when it was just a **sapling.**

trunk

n. 1. The tall main stem of a tree. This is where its branches grow.

On our vacation in California, we saw giant redwood trees with **trunks** almost twenty feet across.

2. The long nose of an elephant.

The elephant lifted its **trunk** in alarm when it heard the motor of the airplane.

3. A large box or case with a lid that can be shut and locked.

Nina opened the **trunk** at the foot of the bed to look for an extra blanket.

4. The covered part at the back of a car. It is used for carrying suitcases and other objects.

Before we leave, will you please put the beach chairs and towels in the **trunk?**

Use your arms to describe a big tree trunk for your partner.

© SSI • DO NOT DUPLICATE

Words and Their Meanings

Look at the group of words next to the number. Then circle the letter next to the word that has the same meaning.

1 the tall main stem of a tree
(a) bud   (b) anchor   (c) core   (d) trunk

2 the hard middle part of a fruit
(a) factory   (b) core   (c) sapling   (d) brush

3 a swelling on a plant that may grow into a flower
(a) brush   (b) sapling   (c) center   (d) bud

4 a building where things are made
(a) factory   (b) center   (c) anchor   (d) hive

5 a weight that holds a boat in place
(a) hive   (b) sapling   (c) anchor   (d) brush

Look at the word next to the number. Then circle the letter next to the group of words that has the same meaning.

| absorb |
| anchor |
| brush |
| bud |
| center |
| core |
| factory |
| hive |
| sapling |
| trunk |
| |

6 center
(a) the highest point   (b) the exact middle
(c) the outside edge   (d) the place where two
                                        things meet

7 sapling
(a) a ripe fruit   (b) a foolish person
(c) a young tree   (d) a young child

8 brush

(a) to land heavily

(b) to touch lightly in passing

(c) to travel very fast

(d) to knock against

9 absorb

(a) to soak up

(b) to give away

(c) to hold in place

(d) to stay behind

10 hive

(a) a home for pigs

(b) a home for birds

(c) a home for horses

(d) a home for bees

5B Seeing Connections

Look at each group of words. Three are related in some way. Find the one word that does not belong and circle it.

1 sail   anchor   brush   motor

2 factory   school   office   beach

3 antenna   branch   leaf   bud

4 airplane   train   trunk   ship

5 peel   flame   core   seeds

© SSI • DO NOT DUPLICATE

5C Applying Meanings

Circle the letter next to the correct answer.

1 Which of the following can **absorb** water?
(a) robot   (b) cloth   (c) rock   (d) steel

2 Which of the following live in a **hive?**
(a) birds   (b) apes   (c) fish   (d) bees

3 Which of the following could be a **sapling?**
(a) an oak   (b) a fish   (c) a daisy   (d) a frog

4 Which of the following has a **center?**
(a) a circle   (b) a smell   (c) a share   (d) a sound

5 Which of the following has a **trunk?**
(a) a bat   (b) a whale   (c) a tree   (d) a daffodil

absorb
anchor
brush
bud
center
core
factory
hive
sapling
trunk

5D

Vocabulary in Context
Read the passage.

The Talking Tree

We know that trees can't talk. But what if they could? They might have some interesting things to tell us. Imagine you are sitting under an apple tree. Then you hear it say something like this.

● ● ● ● ● ● ● ● ● ● ● ●

I'm often asked if I like being a tree. That seems to me a silly question. I don't really have a choice, do I? Right now, I'm only about five feet tall. I'm still a **sapling.** When I'm fully grown, I'll be over twenty feet tall.

Look at me, please. You see only half of me. My roots take up as much space under the ground as my branches do in the air. These roots help me a lot. They keep me **anchored** firmly. They need to be strong. I wouldn't want the wind to blow me over. My roots also give me water. Did you know that I get thirsty just like you do? My roots take water from the soil. The water travels up my **trunk.** Then it goes along each branch into every leaf. During hot, dry weather, I need lots of water just as you do. Without enough water, my leaves turn brown. Then they fall to the ground.

Every one of my leaves is very important. Each is like a little **factory.** First, my leaves take carbon dioxide from the air. Then they mix it with water from my roots. This makes a sugary water. Sugar is a food for trees, just as it is for people. It gives me energy to grow. This sugary water travels from the leaves to feed every part of me. My leaves also help you. The air that you breathe out has more carbon dioxide in it than the air you breathe in. Too much carbon dioxide in the air is bad for people. My leaves **absorb** carbon dioxide. They help keep the air in balance for you. In the early spring, you will see many **buds** starting to grow all over me. Each one will turn into a pink or white flower. Inside these flowers, you'll see a yellow

© SSI • DO NOT DUPLICATE

powder. This is called pollen. Bees fly from flower to flower and collect it from me. Then they take it back to their **hive.** There they use it to feed their young. Something else happens when bees collect pollen. During the collection, some of the pollen from one flower **brushes** against the next one. When this happens, an apple will start to grow from that flower.

There are many different kinds of apple trees. I'm called a Macintosh. My apples will turn red when they're ripe. Other kinds of apples are yellow or even green when they're ripe. In the **center** of each apple, there are little black seeds. You might eat one of my apples and throw the **core** on the ground. Then some of these seeds could grow up to be apple trees just like me.

Answer each of the questions with a sentence.

1 Why does the apple tree say that each of its leaves is like a little **factory?**

_____

_____

2 Why is the **core** a very important part of the apple?

_____

_____

3 In what way are a **sapling** and a child alike?

_____

_____

4 Why is a bee unlikely to fly into a **bud?**

_____

_____

absorb
anchor
brush
bud
center
core
factory
hive
sapling
trunk

5 Why would you expect to see many bees around a **hive** in the early spring?

_____

_____

6 How does the **trunk** of a tree help it stay alive?

_____

_____

7 What will you see if you look into the **center** of a flower?

_____

_____

8 Why do trees need to be firmly **anchored** in the ground by their roots?

_____

_____

9 What could happen to you if you **brush** against flowers on an apple tree?

_____

_____

10 Which part of a tree **absorbs** water?

_____

_____

F**un** FACT

· ·

- Some **anchors** are people. Their job is not to hold a boat in place, though. On TV news shows, the **anchor** is the main person who reports the news.

© SSI · DO NOT DUPLICATE

Vocabulary Extension

core

noun The hard middle part of fruits such as apples or pears.

noun The most important part of something.

Academic Context

Planet Earth has a **core.** Other planets have **cores,** too. The solid inner **core** of Earth is made of iron.

Idioms

to the core Extremely or completely.

Tamika is a dancer to the **core.** *She twirls and leaps everywhere she goes.*

Discussion & Writing Prompt

An apple has a core. What else has a core?

2 min.	3 min.
1. Turn and talk to your partner or group.	2. Write 1–3 sentences.
Use this space to take notes or draw your ideas.	Be ready to share what you have written.

Lesson 5

Review

Hidden Message Write the word that is missing from each sentence in the boxes next to it. The number after a sentence is the lesson the word is from. The shaded boxes will answer this riddle:

What did they call Batman and Robin after the steamroller ran over them?

1. This _____ will grow into a cherry tree. (5)

2. In this _____, they make radios. (5)

3. Gary swam out to the _____ of the lake. (5)

4. The captain raised the _____ and headed out to sea. (5)

5. We live on the _____ Earth. (3)

6. The children are playing tag in the _____. (1)

7. Mom keeps blankets in this old _____. (5)

8. This flower _____ is just beginning to open. (5)

9. The _____ gave us plenty of light. (4)

10. Bees buzzed around the _____. (5)

11. This towel will _____ the water on the floor. (5)

12. Please _____ your teeth now. (5)

13. You can throw away the apple _____. (5)

14. Because of the strong wind, Katie's hair got _____. (2)

© SSI • DO NOT DUPLICATE

Study the words. Then do the exercises that follow.

cone

n. 1. An object that has a round, flat base and comes to a point at the other end.

On their walk to the park, Elena and George each bought a **cone** at the ice-cream stand.

2. The fruit of a pine or other evergreen tree. It holds the seeds.

My sister and I picked up **cones** from our pine tree to make a decoration for the front door.

 Discuss with your partner what a pine cone feels like.

cube

n. A solid figure with six square sides.

We helped Mom by cutting the potatoes into **cubes** for the salad.

 Point to a cube in the classroom with your partner.

Earth

n. 1. The third planet from the sun and the one we live on.

From the spaceship, **Earth** looked like a beautiful giant blue ball.

2. **earth** Soil or dirt.

After planting the tomatoes, Tony smelled the rich, dark **earth.**

 Tell your partner one thing you like about living on Earth.

fern

n. A green plant with feathery leaves. It does not produce flowers.

Josie watched the small spotted frog jump from the path into the bed of **ferns.**

fuel

n. Something that is burned to give power or heat, such as wood, coal, or oil.

Max watched the man who delivers **fuel** as he pulled the hose from his truck to the house next door.

 Tell your partner about how your family uses fuel.

grain

n. 1. A tiny hard piece of something.

With a magnifying glass, we could see that the **grains** of sand had many different colors.

2. The seeds of cereal plants such as corn, wheat, or oats.

By August, many sacks of **grain** stood in a row in the barn.

 Pretend you're dropping grains of sand into your partner's hand.

lizard

n. A cold-blooded animal with a long, narrow body. It has four legs and a long tail.

The **lizard,** which was resting on the large flat stone, didn't move a muscle as Arelis walked by.

© SSI • DO NOT DUPLICATE

miner

n. Someone who works to dig coal or useful minerals out of the ground.

All the **miners** put on their helmets before they went to work.

present

n. 1. The time that is happening now. It is between the past and the future.

The story we are reading takes place in the **present.**

2. Something that one person gives to another to show love, friendship, or thanks.

The **present** I am giving to my friend on her birthday is in the green box with the white ribbon.

adj. Being at a certain place at a certain time. Its opposite is *absent.*

All the students were **present** when the bell rang to start class.

seam

n. 1. The line made when two pieces of cloth are sewn together.

When Luis reached for the ball, he heard his shirt rip at the arm **seam.**

2. A layer of some natural material that lies between two other layers in the ground.

We could see a **seam** of gray clay running through the cliff by the beach.

6A

Completing Sentences

Circle each answer choice that correctly completes the sentence. Each question has three correct answers.

1 **Grains**

(a) such as wheat and oats are the main plants in the field.

(b) of rice were sometimes thrown at weddings.

(c) of sand form the beaches of the world.

(d) are parts of the body that need to be protected.

2 The **seam**

(a) of copper was found two miles underground.

(b) has come apart and needs to be stitched.

(c) rose from the ground and reached a height of a hundred feet.

(d) was sewn so well that you could not see it.

3 A **cube**

(a) with a number on each side is called a die.

(b) is a solid object with six square sides.

(c) allows water to flow through it.

(d) of ice will cool the drink.

4 A **miner's**

(a) workplace is a factory or workshop.

(b) tools include a flashlight and shovel.

(c) job is an especially dirty one.

(d) great fear is probably of being trapped underground.

5 **Ferns**

(a) do not produce flowers.

(b) will run if startled by a sudden noise.

(c) have long feathery leaves.

(d) are mostly green in color.

© SSI • DO NOT DUPLICATE

Making Connections

Circle the letter next to the correct answer.

❶ Which word goes with *ice cream?*
(a) cube   (b) fern   (c) cone   (d) grain

❷ Which word goes with *garden?*
(a) earth   (b) anchor   (c) factory   (d) fuel

❸ Which word goes with *here?*
(a) shelter   (b) joint   (c) present   (d) seam

❹ Which word goes with *tail?*
(a) seam   (b) grain   (c) cube   (d) lizard

❺ Which word goes with *heat?*
(a) fuel   (b) earth   (c) sapling   (d) yard

cone
cube
earth
fern
fuel
grain
lizard
miner
present
seam

Using Context Clues

Circle the letter next to the word that correctly completes the sentence.

1 The _____ was so beautifully sewn you couldn't see it.
(a) seam   (b) lizard   (c) fern   (d) present

2 Wood and coal are used for _____.
(a) earth   (b) grain   (c) fuel   (d) balance

3 A _____ is a green plant with feathery leaves.
(a) fern   (b) sapling   (c) lizard   (d) grain

4 The time between the past and the future is the _____.
(a) flap   (b) flame   (c) cone   (d) present

5 A(n) _____ works underground digging coal.
(a) lizard   (b) miner   (c) acrobat   (d) groom

Vocabulary in Context

Read the passage.

What It's Like to Be 300 Million Years Old

Rocks can't talk, of course. But they can tell a lot to someone who knows how to listen. Let's imagine we can hear what this rock has to say.

• • • • • • • • • • •

Hello, I'm a rock. I'm small enough to fit in your hand. My color is shiny black. Unlike other rocks, I burn easily. Can you guess what kind of rock I am? I am coal.

My story begins 300 million years ago. This was long before the dinosaurs lived. There were few animals on **Earth** then. There were snails, spiders, and small **lizards.** Sharks

© SSI • DO NOT DUPLICATE

swam in the seas. Huge dragonflies and other insects flew through the air.

The weather at that time was warm and rainy. Plants covered the land. **Ferns** were especially common. Some of these grew as large as trees. But there were no plants with flowers. There were also no trees that dropped their leaves in the fall. Pine trees, however, were common. They dropped their **cones** to the ground. Then new trees grew from the cones to take their place. As the trees and plants died, the things growing on top pressed them down into the soil. More layers grew over them. Millions of years passed. These layers of dead plants became many feet thick.

Seas formed over what had been dry land. Countless **grains** of sand fell to the bottom of the sea. The weight of all this sand pressed down on itself. The loose sand changed into sandstone. The sandstone squeezed the layer of dead plants beneath the sand. These dead plants later became a thick **seam** of hard shiny rock. I was part of that rock.

Over several million years, the sea disappeared. It became dry land. Later, the dinosaurs came. Then they died out. During all that time, I was lying deep underground. Then humans appeared. They began living in different places. They wore clothes to keep warm. They made fires out of wood. But before long, the humans discovered that I was a much better **fuel** than wood. I burned hotter and longer. **Miners** went under the ground to dig me out.

Now I'm lying with a bunch of rocks just like me. We're waiting to be burned. Our energy will be used to make electricity. You might wonder what will happen when there are no more layers left in the ground. That won't happen for a long time. At **present,** there are about one trillion tons still in the ground. That's the number one followed by twelve zeroes. This is enough coal to make a **cube** with each side more than a mile long. It's enough to build a wall about 500 feet tall and 500 feet wide from Los Angeles to New York. I think you'll agree that is a lot of coal.

| cone |
| cube |
| earth |
| fern |
| fuel |
| grain |
| lizard |
| miner |
| present |
| seam |

Answer each of the questions with a sentence.

1 How can we tell from the passage that **ferns** do not have flowers?

_____

_____

2 How long has coal been in the **earth?**

_____

_____

3 Why would a new pine grow from a **cone** that fell from the tree?

_____

_____

4 Why would you expect a **seam** of coal to be deep in the ground?

_____

_____

5 What kind of sea creature that was living 300 million years ago is still living in the **present?**

_____

_____

6 How did the **grains** of sand become sandstone?

_____

_____

7 About how much coal would there be in a **cube** with sides more than a mile across?

_____

_____

© SSI • DO NOT DUPLICATE

8 Which lived on Earth first—**lizards** or dinosaurs? Explain your answer.

_____

_____

9 How would **miners** know they had reached a layer of coal?

_____

_____

10 What kind of **fuel** did humans burn before they learned about burning coal?

_____

_____

Fun FACT

- Do you know the difference between **miner** and **minor?**
  A **minor** is a person who is under eighteen years old.

cone
cube
earth
fern
fuel
grain
lizard
miner
present
seam

6 Vocabulary Extension

present

verb To show, tell about, or describe something to another person or group.

noun The time that is happening now.

adjective In a place; not absent.

noun Something that one person gives to another to show love, friendship, or thanks.

Academic Context

In school, when you **present** something, you show information to the class and talk about it.

Word Family

presentable (adjective)

presenter (noun)

presentation (noun)

Discussion & Writing Prompt

Tell about a time you **presented** schoolwork in class.

2 min.	**3 min.**
1. Turn and talk to your partner or group.	**2.** Write 1–3 sentences.
Use this space to take notes or draw your ideas.	Be ready to share what you have written.

© SSI • DO NOT DUPLICATE

Review

Crossword Puzzle Solve the puzzle by writing the missing word in each sentence in the boxes with the matching numbers. The number after each clue is the lesson the word is from.

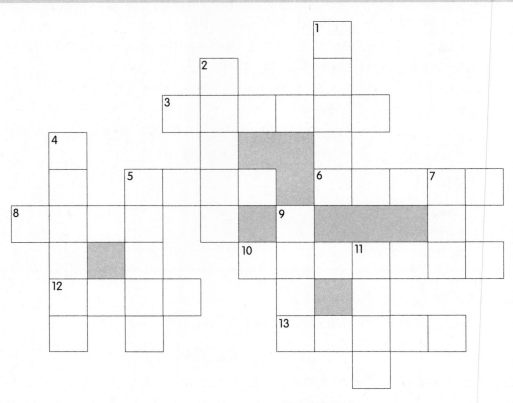

ACROSS

3. The _____ ran under a rock when I came near. (6)

5. Planes do not use the same _____ as cars. (6)

6. The groom is walking the _____ around the track.

8. Victor put a _____ of ice in each glass. (6)

10. Only one student was not _____ when class began. (6)

12. We each bought an ice-cream _____. (6)

13. The wind blew a _____ of sand in my eye. (6)

DOWN

1. The moon is about 240,000 miles from _____. (6)

2. A _____ usually works under the ground. (6)

4. Liz will _____ the ball before she hits it. (2)

5. Many _____ grow by the road in the spring. (6)

7. The _____ rises in the east each morning.

9. The green _____ croaked and hopped away.

11. After it split open, I sewed the _____ closed. (6)

Study the words. Then do the exercises that follow.

badge

n. A sign or mark to show that a person belongs to a certain group.

The police officer pinned the silver **badge** on her shirt before she went to work.

banner

n. A flag or other piece of cloth with words or signs on it.

A **banner** was hanging across the street to announce the spring festival in the park.

corner

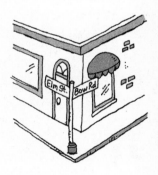

n. 1. The place where two walls or two sides of something meet.

Mom and I pushed my bed to the **corner** of the room so that I could clean the floor.

2. The place where two streets come together.

Jennie, José, and Lee wait for the school bus at the **corner** of Elm Street and Bow Road.

v. To force a person or animal into a place that is hard to get out of.

We **cornered** the puppy by the house and carried him back to his pen.

. . . .

Plan with your partner how you would corner a mouse in the classroom and take it safely outside

© SSI • DO NOT DUPLICATE

design

n. A pattern or arrangement of lines, shapes, or colors.

Kim and Ricky worked on the **design** for the poster to announce the book sale.

v. To make a plan to show how something will look or how it will be made.

Gustavo and I will **design** the puppet theater, and Margot will make one of the puppets.

Talk with your partner about how you would design a poster for your favorite movie.

display

n. A public showing of things so that they can be looked at.

One of my favorite **displays** at the science museum is the one showing shells from all over the world.

v. To set something out for others to see.

The farmers **displayed** corn, beans, and tomatoes at the market on Thursday.

Display the things on the table or desk in front of you for your partner.

fold

n. A mark or crease made when something is bent over on itself.

The direction says to tear the paper along the **fold.**

v. To bend something over one or more times so that one part rests on another.

When the dryer stopped, Min and Lee **folded** the clean towels and socks.

Use a piece of scrap paper to show your partner how to make a fold.

parade

n. Many people marching or moving along together in a line. They do this to enjoy or remember an event. There are often bands, cars, and flags.

Marco and Fran joined the big crowd on the sidewalk to watch the **parade** go by.

rectangle

n. A figure made from four straight lines. All four angles in the figure are the same size.

This green **rectangle** in the center of the map stands for the park near our house.

salute

v. To respect or honor in some way such as by raising the hand to the forehead.

As soon as the president walked into the room, the soldiers **saluted.**

tread

n. The grooved part of a tire that touches the ground as it moves.

Dad was worried when I showed him a smooth place on the **tread.**

v. To walk or step on by bringing the feet down.

When you go up the stairs, please **tread** lightly so that you don't wake up your sisters.

· ·

Show your partner what you tread on in the classroom.

© SSI • DO NOT DUPLICATE

7A

Words and Their Meanings

Look at the group of words next to the number. Then circle the letter next to the word that has the same meaning.

1 many people marching or moving along a certain street
(a) banner   (b) corner   (c) parade   (d) badge

2 a cloth with words or signs on it
(a) fold   (b) banner   (c) salute   (d) tread

3 a figure made with four straight lines and equal angles
(a) corner   (b) design   (c) display   (d) rectangle

4 a place where two streets meet
(a) tread   (b) fold   (c) corner   (d) design

5 a sign to show you belong to a certain group
(a) badge   (b) display   (c) fold   (d) tread

Look at the word next to the number. Then circle the letter next to the group of words that has the same meaning.

6 tread
(a) to move without making a noise   (b) to keep from sinking
(c) to walk or step on   (d) to follow closely

7 fold
(a) to almost lose one's balance   (b) to bend so that one part rests on another
(c) to cut into little pieces   (d) to set out something for others to see

| badge |
| banner |
| corner |
| design |
| display |
| fold |
| parade |
| rectangle |
| salute |
| tread |

8 design

(a) a way that leads to a place

(b) a paper on which you write your name

(c) a memory of something past

(d) a pattern of lines, shapes, or colors

9 salute

(a) to take the lead

(b) to raise the hand as a sign of respect

(c) to come to a complete stop

(d) to go in a different direction

10 display

(a) to set out something for others to see

(b) to enjoy what one is doing

(c) to force something into a place with no escape

(d) to hide something

7B Seeing Connections

Look at each group of words. Three are related in some way. Find the one word that does not belong and circle it.

1 skip   run   tread   fold

2 side   badge   center   corner

3 wave   salute   cry   point

4 display   hide   cover   bury

5 cloth   banner   cone   flag

© SSI • DO NOT DUPLICATE

Applying Meanings

Circle the letter next to the correct answer.

1 On which of the following could you **tread?**

(a) wind   (b) stars   (c) stairs   (d) music

2 Which of the following could have a **fold?**

(a) an egg   (b) a newspaper
(c) a chimney   (d) a nail

3 Which of the following might you see in a **parade?**

(a) cliffs   (b) factories   (c) flags   (d) planets

4 Which of the following could have the shape of a **rectangle?**

(a) a yard   (b) a pebble
(c) a cone   (d) a dozen

5 Which of the following can humans **design?**

(a) the ocean   (b) a cloud
(c) a storm   (d) a motor

badge
banner
corner
design
display
fold
parade
rectangle
salute
tread

Wave to Me, and I'll Wave Back

The United States flag is more than two hundred years old. What if it could talk? Imagine what it has seen. Think about where it has been. Here are some of the things it might tell you.

• • • • • • • • • • • •

I am very old. But that doesn't stop me from getting around. On the Fourth of July, you will see me in **parades** all over this country. You might see me every day at your school. In New York City, at the United Nations Building, I fly with the flags of countries from all over the world.

People call me by different names. One is the Stars and Stripes. Another is the Star-Spangled **Banner.** Often you see me as a cloth **rectangle** flying from the top of a flagpole. Sometimes I'm made of metal and worn as a **badge.** In my top left **corner,** I have fifty white stars arranged on a blue background. There is one star for each state. The rest of me is covered with thirteen stripes. Six are white. Seven are red.

I have not always looked this way. Over the years, I have had different **designs.** One that was very surprising was an early one. I had only red and white stripes. There was a picture of a rattlesnake, too. The words "Don't **Tread** On Me" were written below the snake. This was during the time the Americans were fighting the British. I was a warning to leave America alone. Not long after, I was given thirteen stars and thirteen stripes. That's one for each original state.

My thirteen stripes have stayed the same. But my stars have changed over time. Each time a new state is added, I get a new star. The last stars were for Alaska and Hawaii. They became states in 1959.

© SSI • DO NOT DUPLICATE

I have traveled to many faraway places over the years. In 1840, I was on a boat going to the South Pole with explorers. In 1963, I traveled to the top of Mount Everest with climbers. In 1969, I flew to the moon with astronauts. In these places, I now often fly next to the flags of other countries.

All flags want to be treated well. When you **salute** me, you should stand straight and be serious. If you see me dragging on the ground, please lift me up. When it is night, take me down. Then **fold** me carefully before you put me away. I hope you will **display** me on special days of the year. I especially like June 14, Flag Day. July 4, Independence Day, is a good one, too. Of course, you can fly me every day of the year if you want to. I like to be out in the open air.

Answer each of the questions with a sentence.

1 What is in the small **rectangle** on an American flag?

_____

_____

2 If a **badge** of the American flag has forty-eight stars, when was it made?

_____

_____

3 How should you look when you **salute** the flag of your country?

_____

_____

4 When do Americans **display** the flag?

_____

_____

| badge |
| banner |
| corner |
| design |
| display |
| fold |
| parade |
| rectangle |
| salute |
| tread |

5 What flags would you expect to see waving at a Fourth of July **parade?**

_____

_____

6 If a **corner** of the flag is on the ground, what should you do?

_____

_____

7 Why do you think the flag has to be **folded** before it is put away?

_____

_____

8 Where did the Star-Spangled **Banner** travel in 1969?

_____

_____

9 Why should you never **tread** on the American flag?

_____

_____

10 How has the **design** of the American flag changed over the years?

_____

_____

Fun FACT

• If a day turns out really great, you can say, "This was a **banner** day!" That means something so good happened that you almost want to hang out a **banner** to celebrate it.

© SSI • DO NOT DUPLICATE

Vocabulary Extension

design

noun A pattern of lines, shapes, or colors.

verb To make a plan to show how something will look or how it will be made.

Word Family

designed (verb)

designer (noun)

designing (verb)

Discussion & Writing Prompt

My mom is the designer of the new skateboard.

A **designer** plans how something is made or will look. Tell about something you want to **design.**

`2 min.`	`3 min.`
1. Turn and talk to your partner or group.	**2.** Write 1–3 sentences.
Use this space to take notes or draw your ideas.	Be ready to share what you have written.

Review

Hidden Message Write the word that is missing from each sentence in the boxes next to it. The number after each sentence is the lesson the word is from. The shaded boxes will answer this riddle:

Where does today come before yesterday?

. . . .

1. At the science fair, students will _____ their projects. (7)

2. We put the floor lamp in the _____ of the room, where it won't be knocked over. (7)

. . . .

3. The shape of a dollar bill is a _____. (7)

4. We heard a heavy _____ on the stairs near our room. (7)

H

. . . .

5. This small metal _____ shows the country's flag. (7)

6. The _____ of a chessboard is very simple. (7)

7. From the top of the _____, we could see the ocean. (3)

8. The soldier _____ the general. (7)

9. White smoke poured out of the _____. (4)

10. Now _____ the paper in half. (7)

11. Our school _____ hangs in the gym. (7)

12. A marching band led the _____. (7)

13. My sister and I _____ this bicycle. (1)

Y

© SSI • DO NOT DUPLICATE

Study the words. Then do the exercises that follow.

aquarium

n. 1. A glass tank filled with water. Plants and animals that live in water, especially fish, are kept there.

Sophie loved to watch the brightly colored clown fish swim in her **aquarium.**

2. A building where many different kinds of living fish and other water animals are on display.

In the center of the **aquarium** stands a huge glass tank where hundreds of fish, eels, and turtles swim.

cage

n. A kind of box with bars or wire netting. It is a place to keep animals or birds.

My canary flew into the kitchen when my cousin opened the door of its **cage.**

Tell your partner about something that lives in a cage.

club

n. 1. A heavy stick that is used for hitting and swinging at something.

Long ago, people used **clubs** to protect themselves.

2. A group of people who meet from time to time to do some special thing.

Our **club** meets every week in our clubhouse.

Talk with your partner about a club you want to start at school.

faucet

n. A handle fitted to a pipe. It is used to control the flow of water.

We can get water from the **faucet** at the back of the house to water the garden.

flood

n. A great flow of water over land that is dry.

The **flood** rose to the roofs of the houses on this street.

v. To cover with water.

When the pipe broke, water **flooded** the basement.

 Discuss with your partner what you would do if water flooded the classroom.

gift

n. Something that is given. It is a present.

We often bring my grandmother a **gift** when we stay at her house for a few days.

 Tell your partner about the best gift you ever gave anyone.

icicle

n. A thin, pointed, hanging piece of ice. It is formed by water freezing as it drips.

The **icicles** hanging from the roof sparkled in the bright sunlight.

imitate

v. To try to act like someone or something else.

Maria tried to **imitate** the way her swimming teacher kicked her legs.

 Ask your partner to imitate you as you make funny faces.

© SSI • DO NOT DUPLICATE

pearl

> *n.* A smooth round object that forms inside the shell of an oyster. It is used in jewelry.
>
> When the diver opened the oyster, she saw a **pearl** lying inside the shell.

valley

> *n.* A low piece of land lying between hills or mountains.
>
> On the other side of the **valley,** we could see a line of hills.

8A Completing Sentences

Circle each answer choice that correctly completes the sentence. Each question has three correct answers.

❶ An icicle

(a) tastes sweet because of the sugar in it.

(b) is formed by water as it drips and freezes.

(c) can cause an accident if it falls on you.

(d) grows slowly over time.

❷ The faucet

(a) handle is turned to control the flow of water.

(b) is formed in deep underground seams.

(c) needs to be fixed because it's leaking.

(d) is marked with an *H* for "hot water."

aquarium
cage
club
faucet
flood
gift
icicle
imitate
pearl
valley

3 The **gift**

(a) came with a red ribbon tied around it.

(b) arrived on my birthday and was a total surprise.

(c) is the hard middle part of certain fruits.

(d) was so big, I didn't know what it could be.

4 The **valley**

(a) was wheeled into the room and left there.

(b) was formed by the river that runs through it.

(c) is easily flooded when the water level rises.

(d) is cooler in summer than the higher ground.

5 The **aquarium**

(a) holds several kinds of saltwater fish.

(b) brings water over a hundred miles to the city.

(c) is my favorite place to go to see sharks.

(d) holds fifty gallons of water.

8B

Making Connections

Circle the letter next to the correct answer.

1 Which word goes with *weapon?*

(a) bud   (b) miner   (c) club   (d) aquarium

2 Which word goes with *ape?*

(a) imitate   (b) trunk   (c) pearl   (d) support

3 Which word goes with *wire bars?*

(a) icicle   (b) cage   (c) club   (d) faucet

© SSI • DO NOT DUPLICATE

4 Which word goes with *necklace?*

(a) parade   (b) seam   (c) icicle   (d) pearl

5 Which word goes with *water?*

(a) flame   (b) cage   (c) flood   (d) chimney

8C Using Context Clues

Circle the letter next to the word that correctly completes the sentence.

1 Water flows out of a(n) _____.

(a) faucet   (b) flood   (c) aquarium   (d) factory

2 The _____ was caused by heavy rain.

(a) tangle   (b) flame   (c) flood   (d) icicle

3 You can make a(n) _____ out of heavy wood.

(a) club   (b) desert   (c) pearl   (d) anchor

4 You might find a _____ in an oyster if you are lucky.

(a) bud   (b) banner   (c) club   (d) pearl

5 The _____ melted when the sun came out.

(a) pearl   (b) icicle   (c) motor   (d) fern

aquarium
cage
club
faucet
flood
gift
icicle
imitate
pearl
valley

Get Close to Mother Nature

Nature is all around us—the plants, animals, insects, birds, storms, and sunny weather. Let's imagine that nature could talk to us. What do you think it might tell us?

• • • • • • • • • • • •

Do you know where to find me? Just look around. I am everywhere. I get the blame for storms at sea and **floods** on land. But I am also thanked for many things. The fresh fruits and vegetables you eat come from me. So does the rain that washes the earth and the rainbow that follows after. I am everything you see in the world. Except for the things made by people, of course. The mountains and clouds, rivers and **valleys,** plants and animals, **icicles** and snowflakes are all a part of me. Some people say that they are my **gifts** to the world.

Here's something that might surprise you. Until several thousand years ago, I had the world pretty much to myself. There were very few people then. They had not started to build cities and roads. There were no televisions, no cars, and no computers. People took water from streams or ponds, not from **faucets.** They needed me to stay alive.

Humans, however, are very clever. They liked to **imitate** me. They soon began making things themselves. Take flowers, for example. They made plastic flowers to look like real ones. This is fine, I suppose, if you have a plastic nose. Now humans make trees and grass. They even make **pearls** that look like mine. There is a difference, however. These things often don't feel or smell or taste the same as mine. That is because they aren't real.

Today many people live in apartments, ride buses, and take the subway. They travel in trains, planes, or cars. They don't see me very much. They don't plant seeds. They don't take their food from the earth. Instead, they eat things that come frozen, boxed, or canned. They cut down the trees, which give the

© SSI • DO NOT DUPLICATE

birds a place to live. They cover the fields with parking lots and buildings. They throw their trash all over me. The world has changed so much. Many people don't even know who I am.

Are you one of them? If so, here are a few things you can do to get to know me better. Make an **aquarium.** Just as I take care of life in the rivers, lakes, and seas, you can watch over your fish, turtles, and plants. Start looking at the birds that live near you. Listen to their calls. Learn more about them by joining a bird-watching **club,** not by keeping one in a **cage.** Plant a tree near your school or your home. Work with your class to clean up trash where you live and play. Go barefoot on a sandy beach. You could even walk in the mud at low tide. Feel the mud squeeze between your toes. Lie on your back in a grassy field. Watch the clouds overhead. Then you will know who I am.

Answer each of the questions with a sentence.

1 How did people get their water before they had **faucets?**

_____

_____

2 What is a **club** you might enjoy joining? Why?

_____

_____

3 How do you think living in a **valley** would be different from living on a mountain?

_____

_____

4 Why are wild berries a **gift** from nature?

_____

_____

| aquarium |
| cage |
| club |
| faucet |
| flood |
| gift |
| icicle |
| imitate |
| pearl |
| valley |

5 What is an example of people trying to **imitate** nature?

_____

_____

6 Why is a **flood** a dangerous part of nature?

_____

_____

7 What is the difference between **pearls** made by nature and those made by humans?

_____

_____

8 What are some things you could learn about nature by having an **aquarium** or by visiting one?

_____

_____

9 Why do you think nature does not want you to keep birds in **cages?**

_____

_____

10 What do rain and **icicles** have in common?

_____

_____

Fun
FACT

· ·

- The first part of **aquarium**—*aqua*—means the "greenish-blue color of seawater." *Aqua* is also a lot like the Spanish word for water, *agua*.

© SSI · DO NOT DUPLICATE

Vocabulary **E**xtension

imitate

verb To try to act like someone or something else.

Word Family
imitation (noun)
imitator (noun)

Context Clues
These sentences give clues to the meaning of **imitate.**

> To **imitate** a bird, you can flap your arms and say, "Tweet, tweet!"

> Jamal and Louie jumped and raced, trying to **imitate** their favorite skateboarder.

Discussion & Writing Prompt
Describe how you would **imitate** a bird.

2 min.	3 min.
1. Turn and talk to your partner or group.	**2.** Write 1–3 sentences.
Use this space to take notes or draw your ideas.	Be ready to share what you have written.

Review

Crossword Puzzle Solve the puzzle by writing the missing word in each sentence in the boxes with the matching numbers. The number after each clue is the lesson the word is from.

ACROSS

4. When you visit an _____, you expect to see fish. (8)

5. After the snowstorm, a thick _____ hung from the roof. (8)

7. At school, I belong to the nature _____. (8)

9. The necklace had one small _____. (8)

10. This birthday _____ is just what I wanted. (8)

11. The opposite of *after* is _____.

DOWN

1. We need to fix the _____ so it won't drip. (8)

2. Between the mountains is a _____ with a small town. (8)

3. My friend can _____ the sound of a cardinal perfectly. (8)

6. The heavy rains caused the streets to _____. (8)

7. This _____ is not large enough for two rabbits. (8)

8. The opposite of *top* is _____.

© SSI · DO NOT DUPLICATE

Study the words. Then do the exercises that follow.

aboard

>*adv., prep.* In or on a ship, train, or airplane.
>
>Jason jumped **aboard** the train just before the doors closed.

blast

>*n.* 1. A strong wind or movement of air.
>
>An icy **blast** blew into the room when Caleb opened the door.
>
>2. A loud noise.
>
>The whistle gave two **blasts,** and then the ship began to move away from the dock.
>
>*v.* 1. To blow something up.
>
>To begin making the tunnel through the mountain, the workers need to **blast** these rocks.
>
>2. (*used with* off) To go up in the air or into space.
>
>Raisa and her family will watch the rocket **blast** off at noon tomorrow.

. . . .

Blow through your mouth to show your partner what a blast sounds like.

career

>*n.* The kind of work a person does for many years.
>
>After finishing college, Ramona chose a **career** as a firefighter.

cautious

adj. Careful in order to avoid mistakes, trouble, or danger.

Ray and Theresa were **cautious** when they saw the icy sidewalk.

 Tell your partner one thing to be cautious about on the playground.

girder

n. A large, strong piece of metal or wood used to support bridges or buildings.

These steel **girders** support the railroad bridge.

invent

v. To make something for the first time.

In 1868, Margaret Knight **invented** a machine to make square bottoms on paper bags.

inventor *n.* A person who thinks up or makes something for the first time.

The **inventor** of the electric light bulb was Thomas Edison.

 Talk to your partner about something you want to invent.

rotate

v. 1. To turn in a circle around a center.

Our planet, Earth, **rotates** like a spinning top.

2. To take turns in a certain order.

Miss Wu **rotates** the job of group leader to a different student each week.

 Stand up and show your partner how you can rotate.

© SSI • DO NOT DUPLICATE

story

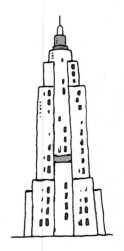

n. 1. A report of something that happened.

A **story** about the science fair at our school was in the newspaper on Tuesday.

2. A tale that is made up. It is often written down for people to read.

Katha is reading a **story** about a mouse named Stuart Little.

3. The space or rooms that make up one level of a building.

The Empire State Building in New York has 102 **stories.**

strand

n. One of the threads that are twisted together to make string, yarn, or rope. It is also a single hair.

The oriole pulled a **strand** from the brush and flew off to its nest.

v. To leave in a difficult or helpless position.

The snowstorm **stranded** my aunt and uncle at the airport for twelve hours.

Tell your partner what you would do if you were stranded on an island.

tower

n. A building or a part of a building that is taller than it is wide.

During our visit to Paris, France, we walked up 360 steps to reach the first level of the Eiffel **Tower.**

v. To rise high in the air.

At five feet, Theo **towers** over his baby sister.

9A Words and Their Meanings

Look at the group of words next to the number. Then circle the letter next to the word that has the same meaning.

1 a loud noise

(a) strand   (b) blast   (c) girder   (d) inventor

2 a metal support

(a) girder   (b) story   (c) tower   (d) strand

3 to make for the first time

(a) tower   (b) rotate   (c) blast   (d) invent

4 job done for years

(a) strand   (b) career   (c) story   (d) tower

5 one level of a building

(a) inventor   (b) strand   (c) story   (d) tower

Look at the word next to the number. Then circle the letter next to the group of words that has the same meaning.

6 aboard

(a) in a helpless state   (b) left behind

(c) going in a circle   (d) on a ship

7 cautious

(a) avoiding mistakes   (b) getting hurt

(c) taking risks   (d) speaking loudly

© SSI • DO NOT DUPLICATE

8 rotate

(a) stay in one place

(b) jump into the air

(c) fall quickly

(d) go in a circle

9 tower

(a) a twisted thread

(b) a tall building

(c) a news report

(d) a strong wind

10 strand

(a) move quickly

(b) blow up

(c) leave in a helpless position

(d) send to the wrong place

9B Seeing Connections

Look at each group of words. Three are related in some way. Find the one word that does not belong and circle it.

1	girder	road	path	track
2	circle	rotate	turn	wave
3	chimney	roof	boat	tower
4	cautious	careful	watchful	foolish
5	tie	strand	fasten	knot

aboard
blast
career
cautious
girder
invent
rotate
story
strand
tower

9c

Applying Meanings

Circle the letter next to the correct answer.

1 Which of the following can be a **career?**

(a) relaxing   (b) dreaming   (c) sleeping   (d) teaching

2 Which of the following was not **invented?**

(a) the ocean   (b) the telephone

(c) the can opener   (d) the light bulb

3 Which of the following can you go **aboard?**

(a) a cavern   (b) a sailboat   (c) a school   (d) a shoe

4 Where will you not find a **story?**

(a) in a library   (b) in a newspaper

(c) in an orange   (d) in a tall building

5 Which of the following can make a **blast?**

(a) a horn   (b) a pillow   (c) a feather   (d) a carrot

© SSI • DO NOT DUPLICATE

Going Around in Circles

Do you like to ride Ferris wheels? Let us explore one of the biggest ones in the world. It is in London, England. It was built to mark the year 2000.

• • • • • • • • • • • •

This giant wheel stands almost 450 feet high. It is in the center of the city next to the Thames River. From a distance, it looks like a great bicycle wheel. The wheel **rotates** very slowly. It does not even seem to be moving. There are thirty-two cars. Each one can carry about two dozen people. The riders have plenty of time to enjoy the views of London. It takes fifteen minutes for each car to go from the ground up to the highest point. At the top, people can see things as far away as twenty-five miles. Maybe that is why this huge wheel is named the London Eye.

The wheel opened in January 2000. More than a million people visited it. Those going **aboard** were not afraid. People know that these giant wheels are very safe. That was not always the case. When it was **invented,** the Ferris wheel scared people.

The year was 1893. The place was the Chicago World's Fair. The people planning the fair wanted something special and surprising to draw a crowd. They chose the design of George Ferris. He had built many bridges in his **career.** His idea was very different. Ferris planned to make a huge steel wheel supported by two tall **towers.** The power from two steam engines would turn the wheel. There would be thirty-six cars. Each could hold sixty people. The wheel would slowly carry people high in the air. Then it would return them to the ground. This looked like fun. But was it safe?

At first, people were **cautious.** The wheel was very high. Chicago already had buildings that were ten **stories** high. But George Ferris's wheel was going to be at least two times as high. In addition, Chicago often had very strong winds.

aboard
blast
career
cautious
girder
invent
rotate
story
strand
tower

Maybe the powerful winds would shake the wheel. What if it twisted out of shape? Could the people in the cars be **stranded** if the engines stopped?

George Ferris believed his wheel was safe. He decided to prove this to everyone. Ferris, his wife, and a brave newspaper reporter chose a windy day to take a ride. Winds were blowing at 110 miles per hour. The three riders stepped into one of the cars. They were slowly carried up into the storm. Later, the reporter wrote that the **blast** from the wind made it impossible to hear. It screamed through the thin **girders.** It shook the windows. But all three returned safely to the ground.

The first Ferris wheel became a very popular ride. Thousands of people rode it all through that summer. Before long, more wheels were built. And they kept getting bigger. At 550 feet, the High Roller in Las Vegas currently holds the world record. But you can bet it won't hold the record for long!

Answer each of the questions with a sentence.

. . . .

1 When did George Ferris **invent** his wheel?

_____

_____

2 Why did people not need to be **cautious** about riding the London Eye in 2000?

_____

_____

3 Why did people think they might be **stranded** on Ferris's wheel?

_____

_____

4 How did George Ferris spend most of his **career?**

_____

_____

© SSI • DO NOT DUPLICATE

5 How did the **blast** of wind affect Ferris's ride?

_____

_____

6 Why is it correct to say that Ferris's wheel **towered** over Chicago?

_____

_____

7 How many people went **aboard** the Ferris wheel during the Chicago World's Fair?

_____

_____

8 How long does it take for the London Eye to **rotate** once?

_____

_____

9 What do you think the **girders** of Ferris's wheel were made of?

_____

_____

10 How many **stories** taller was Ferris's wheel than the tallest buildings in Chicago in 1893?

_____

_____

| aboard |
| blast |
| career |
| cautious |
| girder |
| invent |
| rotate |
| story |
| strand |
| tower |

Fun FACT

• By moving the _r_ in **aboard**, you have a new word— **abroad**. Abroad means "far away from home in another country." You can go **aboard** a ship to travel **abroad.**

inventor

noun A person who thinks up or makes something for the first time.

. . . .

Academic Context

In school, you can learn about different **inventors.** For example, Alexander Graham Bell invented the telephone.

Word Family

invent (verb)

invented (verb)

invention (noun)

Discussion & Writing Prompt

If you were an **inventor,** what would you invent?

2 min.	3 min.
1. Turn and talk to your partner or group.	**2.** Write 1–3 sentences.
Use this space to take notes or draw your ideas.	Be ready to share what you have written.

© SSI • DO NOT DUPLICATE

Review

Crossword Puzzle Solve the puzzle by writing the missing word in each sentence in the boxes with the matching numbers. The number after each clue is the lesson the word is from.

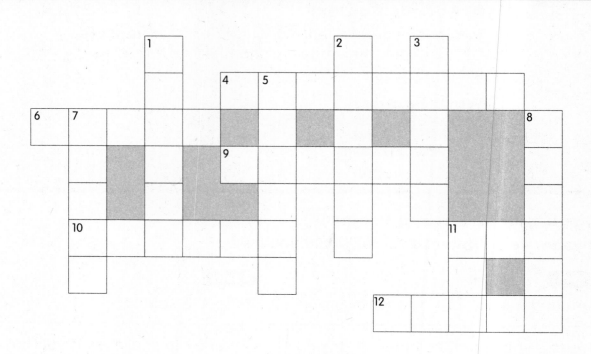

ACROSS

4. Be _____ when you cross this busy street. (9)

6. The _____ tells how Mister Toad got lost in the woods. (9)

9. The wheels on the bus _____ when it moves. (9)

10. A _____ in nursing can be very rewarding. (9)

11. You _____ with your eyes.

12. Three, two, one, _____ off! (9)

DOWN

1. The _____ supports one end of the bridge. (9)

2. Each _____ in this silk cord is a different color. (9)

3. These giant redwoods _____ over the other trees. (9)

5. We went _____ the ship at noon. (9)

7. Mr. Grove wants to _____ second grade.

8. Jon wants to _____ a better mousetrap. (9)

11. Rivers empty into the _____.

Study the words. Then do the exercises that follow.

astronomy

n. The study of planets, stars, and space.

Many people who take up **astronomy** first became interested when they were children.

astronomer *n.* A person who studies astronomy.

An **astronomer** uses a telescope to study space.

. . . .

Discuss with your partner what you could learn using astronomy.

besides

prep. In addition to or also.

Besides being on the soccer team, Sean loves playing basketball.

crater

n. A hole in the shape of a bowl found in the ground or at the mouth of a volcano.

The hikers walked to the top of the volcano to look down into the large **crater.**

degree

n. 1. A unit for measuring how warm something is.

Cindy heated the oven to 350 **degrees** before she put the bread in to bake.

2. A stage or step in a series.

By **degrees,** Malcolm slowly got better at doing his math problems.

. . . .

Move toward your partner by small degrees.

© SSI • DO NOT DUPLICATE

diameter

n. The distance from side to side and through the center of a circle or a round object.

The **diameter** of the trunk of our old oak tree was at least thirty inches.

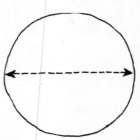

 Draw a circle on a piece of scrap paper and then show your partner where the diameter is.

gaze

v. To look steadily at something for a long time.

Sam and Julie **gazed** at the polar bears swimming in a large pool at the zoo.

gravity

n. 1. The force that pulls things toward the center of Earth.

Gravity causes an apple to fall to the ground.

2. The condition of being serious.

Celia understood later the **gravity** of what she had done by playing too close to the large waves.

 Show your partner how your face looks when you think about something of gravity.

reflect

v. 1. To turn or throw back, such as light or sound.

The mirror **reflected** Tyler's face when he looked into it.

2. To think carefully about something.

Paul **reflected** on the next chess piece he would move.

 Tell your partner what you might reflect on when you write a poem.

telescope

n. An object that makes distant things seem closer and larger. It does this by using mirrors and lenses.

On a cool October night, Dad and Molly set up the **telescope** in the backyard to view the stars.

universe

n. All of space and all the objects in space.

The Milky Way is just one of many large groups of stars in our **universe.**

10A Completing Sentences

Circle each answer choice that correctly completes the sentence. Each question has three correct answers.

❶ There was no one in the room **besides**

(a) the Fourth of July.

(b) the teacher.

(c) Darryl and his silly cat.

(d) my grandfather, who was asleep.

❷ **Craters**

(a) are formed when large objects from space hit Earth.

(b) on the surface of Mars can be seen with a telescope.

(c) are Milo's favorite food, and he says they are healthy.

(d) soon fill with water if they are not filled in with dirt.

© SSI • DO NOT DUPLICATE

3 The **universe**

(a) is full of millions of stars.

(b) is so big, I don't know where it might end.

(c) is all around our planet.

(d) is the smallest animal in the world.

4 **Degrees** measure

(a) how warm something is.

(b) the temperature of the oven.

(c) the diameter of an apple.

(d) the different steps in a series.

5 **Astronomers** teach us that

(a) none of the planets are real.

(b) our sun is just another star.

(c) Jupiter is the largest planet in our solar system.

(d) the Milky Way contains billions of stars.

astronomy
besides
crater
degree
diameter
gaze
gravity
reflect
telescope
universe

Making Connections
Circle the letter next to the correct answer.

1. Which word goes with *stars?*
   (a) machine   (b) telescope   (c) antenna   (d) crater

2. Which word goes with *circle?*
   (a) dozen   (b) reflect   (c) gravity   (d) diameter

3. Which word goes with *serious?*
   (a) gravity   (b) invent   (c) degree   (d) girder

4. Which word goes with *stare?*
   (a) invent   (b) design   (c) gaze   (d) reflect

5. Which word goes with *think?*
   (a) gaze   (b) rotate   (c) imitate   (d) reflect

Using Context Clues
Circle the letter next to the word that correctly completes the sentence.

1. The water _____ the full moon.
   (a) absorbed   (b) reversed   (c) reflected   (d) flapped

2. Kendall's interest in _____ led her to become an astronaut.
   (a) astronomy   (b) degrees   (c) lizards   (d) factories

3. _____ French, Carlos is also studying Spanish.
   (a) Reflecting   (b) Besides   (c) Imitating   (d) Inventing

© SSI • DO NOT DUPLICATE

4 Marco could see the moon's craters clearly through the _____.
    (a) universe   (b) cavern   (c) scoop   (d) telescope

5 The temperature fell to zero _____.
    (a) strands   (b) degrees   (c) diameters   (d) centers

10D Vocabulary in Context
Read the passage.

Twinkle, Twinkle, Little Star

How far up does the sky go? It seems to go on forever. No one knows where space ends. No one even knows if it has an end. So let us explore a small piece of it, our system of planets.

People have always **gazed** at the night sky. Long ago, they saw the moon and the stars just as we do today. But some people noticed something more. They saw that some stars moved slowly across the night sky. Now we know that the moving objects are not stars at all. They are planets circling the sun.

About five billion years ago, the sun and planets were formed. They were made from clouds of gas and dust. **Gravity** pulled the chunks and pieces together to make lumps of matter. More and more dust was added to them. This made the lumps get bigger. The largest lump became the sun. It is a giant star. It shines brightly because it is an enormous ball of fire. Eight smaller lumps circle the sun. These are the planets. They **reflect** light from the sun.

The four planets farthest from the sun are Neptune, Uranus, Saturn, and Jupiter. No astronaut will ever land on any of these four. That is because they are made of gas. Each of these planets has rings around it. Each planet also has several moons. Jupiter is the largest planet. Its **diameter** is eleven times that of the Earth.

astronomy
besides
crater
degree
diameter
gaze
gravity
reflect
telescope
universe

Four smaller planets are closer to the sun. They are Mars, Earth, Venus, and Mercury. All of them are made of solid rock. Mercury is the closest to the sun. It is very hot. The temperature there can rise to 840 **degrees.** That's almost twice as high as the top setting on an oven!

About four hundred years ago, the **telescope** was invented. People were able to look closely at the planets for the first time. The early **astronomers** were surprised. Saturn's rings were beautiful. Mars had huge **craters.** Jupiter had several moons. One of the moons was even bigger than Mercury.

Our planet Earth travels around the sun. It is on a path between those of Mars and Venus. We think that Earth is one of the few planets in the **universe** that has liquid water. Our distance from the sun gives us just the right amount of heat. If we were much closer, the oceans would boil away. If we were much farther away, the oceans would turn to ice. But the temperature is just right. So life in all of its forms is possible on Earth.

Scientists now know that there are other suns **besides** our own. These suns also have planets circling them. They are very, very far away. Is there life on any of them? We do not know. They might have creatures that are smarter than we can imagine. Or Earth may be the only planet anywhere that has life. As more of space is explored, we may someday find out.

Answer each of the questions with a sentence.

1 According to the passage, which planet **besides** Earth has living creatures on it?

_____

_____

2 What did some of the very first **astronomers** see in the night sky?

_____

_____

© SSI • DO NOT DUPLICATE

③ What would you see if you were **gazing** at Saturn?

_____

_____

④ What did **gravity** pull together to make the sun and planets?

_____

_____

⑤ Why will we probably not find any **craters** on the four giant planets?

_____

_____

⑥ Do you think there might be other life in the **universe?** Explain your answer.

_____

_____

⑦ Which details in the passage tell you that the planets formed by **degrees?**

_____

_____

astronomy
besides
crater
degree
diameter
gaze
gravity
reflect
telescope
universe

⑧ How does the **diameter** of Jupiter compare with that of Earth?

_____

_____

⑨ Why is it incorrect to say that the sun **reflects** light?

_____

_____

⑩ How did the invention of the **telescope** help science?

_____

_____

Fun FACT

- **Besides** and **beside** look almost the same but have very different meanings. As you just learned, **besides** means "in addition to, or also." **Beside** means "next to." Be careful to use these words correctly, or you may say something you do not mean. For example:

*Melanie ate two scoops of ice cream **beside** the table.*

*Melanie ate two scoops of ice cream **besides** the table.*

(She must have had a bad stomachache after that meal!)

© SSI • DO NOT DUPLICATE

reflect

verb To think carefully about something.

verb To turn or throw back, such as light or sound.

Academic Context

When you **reflect** on something you have learned, you think carefully about it.

Word Family

reflection (noun)

reflecting (adjective)

reflector (noun)

Discussion & Writing Prompt

Reflect on one thing you learned today and tell about it.

2 min.	**3 min.**
1. Turn and talk to your partner or group.	**2.** Write 1–3 sentences.
Use this space to take notes or draw your ideas.	Be ready to share what you have written.

Lesson 10

Review

Hidden Message Write the word that is missing from each sentence in the boxes next to it. All the words are from Lesson 10. The shaded boxes will answer this riddle:

**Darryl has two coins that equal thirty cents.
One of them is not a nickel. How can that be?**

1. That photo clearly shows a _____ on the moon.

2. A circle is divided into two equal parts by its _____.

H

3. The _____ discovered a new star.

4. People on a spaceship do not feel any _____.

5. The water will _____ the sunlight into your eyes.

6. The temperature dropped to thirty _____ last night.

H

7. Earth is only a very tiny part of the _____.

8. We wanted to _____ at the stars all night.

O

9. _____ Jill, I have two other sisters.

10. Through the _____, we could see Venus.

© SSI • DO NOT DUPLICATE

Word List

Study the words. Then do the exercises that follow.

atlas

n. A book of maps.

To find the Ganges River, Ben used an **atlas.**

aware

adj. Knowing of or about something.

Stacey was not **aware** that she had left her notebook at school until she got home and looked in her backpack.

Tell your partner about a sound you are aware of in your classroom.

boar

n. An adult male pig.

At night, wild **boars** hunt in the forest for roots.

equator

n. An imaginary line around the middle of Earth. It is at an equal distance from the North and South Poles.

If you live near the **equator,** you will notice that the length of the days and nights is almost equal.

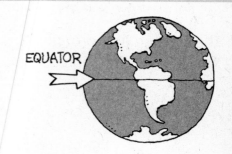

fang

n. A long pointed tooth. It is found in animals like dogs and tigers, which use it to tear meat. It is also found in snakes.

When the tiger opened its mouth to roar, we could see its **fangs** clearly.

fierce

adj. 1. Wild and likely to attack.

A polar bear in the wild may become **fierce** if it is hungry.

2. Very strong and violent.

A **fierce** wind blew sand into Keith's face as he walked home along the beach.

 Show your partner what you look like when you act fierce.

hoof

n. The hard, tough covering on the foot of an animal such as a horse, a cow, or a deer.

Lydia carefully removed the stone from her horse's **hoof.**

journey

n. A long trip from one place to another.

Last summer, our family made a **journey** across Canada by train.

 Tell your partner about a journey you want to take.

local

adj. Having to do with a particular place. It is usually the town or neighborhood where one lives.

Yesterday, Hanna and I picked two quarts of strawberries at a **local** farm.

 Tell your partner about a local place you like to visit.

© SSI • DO NOT DUPLICATE

rare

adj. 1. Not seen or happening very often.

Looking through the book of **rare** butterflies, Leanne showed Mr. Bonilla one of her favorites.

2. Cooked very little.

Eating **rare** meat may not be good for your health.

Discuss with your partner something that is rare about where you live.

11A Words and Their Meanings

Look at the group of words next to the number. Then circle the letter next to the word that has the same meaning.

❶ a tooth used for tearing meat

(a) hoof　　　(b) atlas　　　(c) fang　　　(d) boar

❷ a hard covering on the foot of a cow

(a) boar　　　(b) hoof　　　(c) journey　　　(d) local

❸ a book of maps

(a) atlas　　　(b) local　　　(c) equator　　　(d) journey

❹ a grown male pig

(a) equator　　　(b) journey　　　(c) boar　　　(d) local

❺ a long trip

(a) rare　　　(b) equator　　　(c) local　　　(d) journey

atlas
aware
boar
equator
fang
fierce
hoof
journey
local
rare

6 fierce

   (a) ready to attack   (b) acting silly

   (c) feeling sad   (d) being careful

7 equator

   (a) an imaginary line from the North to the South Pole

   (b) an imaginary line around the middle of Earth

   (c) an imaginary line to the bottom of the ocean

   (d) an imaginary line at the very top of Earth

8 local

   (a) not sure or certain   (b) taking place often

   (c) high in the air   (d) close to where one lives

9 aware

   (a) knowing something   (b) looking for a long time

   (c) making something new   (d) being without help

10 rare

   (a) easy to find   (b) turning in circles

   (c) not happening often   (d) hard to follow

© SSI • DO NOT DUPLICATE

11B Seeing Connections

Look at each group of words. Three are related in some way. Find the one word that does not belong and circle it.

1. local   boar   city   home

2. journey   trip   rare   train

3. atlas   lion   fierce   attack

4. pig   hog   aware   boar

5. fast   local   speedy   rapid

11C Applying Meanings

Circle the letter next to the correct answer.

1. Which of the following will make you **aware** of smoke?
   (a) elbow   (b) ears   (c) nose   (d) teeth

2. Which of the following does not have **fangs?**
   (a) a tiger   (b) a bee   (c) a snake   (d) a wolf

3. Where are you most likely to find **fierce** animals?
   (a) in a jungle   (b) at a subway   (c) in a house   (d) on a farm

4. Which would tell you that you are near the **equator?**
   (a) day is longer than night all year
   (b) days and nights are very cold all year
   (c) night is longer than day all year
   (d) day and night are always the same length

5. Which of the following are **rare** in a school?
   (a) desks   (b) erasers   (c) dogs   (d) students

| atlas |
| aware |
| boar |
| equator |
| fang |
| fierce |
| hoof |
| journey |
| local |
| rare |

Watch Out for Dragons

Where do you find dragons? Many people will say only in storybooks. But there is a real place where dragons live. It is the island of Komodo. So let us go explore.

• • • • • • • • • • • •

First, we must find it. In an **atlas,** look up Indonesia. This is a large country north of Australia. It has thousands of islands. Komodo is one of the smaller ones. It is about six hundred miles south of the **equator.** The dragons that live on Komodo are very **fierce.** They are protected and live in Komodo National Park.

In storybooks, dragons are large creatures. They breathe fire. They have wings, sharp **fangs,** and claws. Of course, they are imaginary. The Komodo dragons are actually lizards. They do not have wings. Their long yellow tongues look like flames only when they shoot out and test the air for smells. These creatures are very big. They may grow to be ten feet in length. And they can weigh two hundred pounds or more. In fact, they are the largest lizards now living on Earth. They have long lives. Many live to be over thirty years old.

The people on the island stay away from these hungry hunters. An adult Komodo dragon has an enormous appetite when it has not eaten for several days. This is when it is most dangerous. It will look for a place to hide. Often, it chooses a place near a trail that other animals walk on. Then it waits. It keeps very still. If it is lucky, a deer, a wild **boar,** or a snake will come close. By the time the animal becomes **aware** of any danger, it is too late. The Komodo dragon leaps quickly from its hiding place. It bites the creature with its sharp teeth. Then it knocks it to the ground. The large lizard usually eats almost everything. It even eats bones, **hooves,** and skin. It can finish a meal in twenty minutes.

© SSI • DO NOT DUPLICATE

Did the idea for storybook dragons come from the dragons of Komodo? It is not likely. Only the people living on Komodo knew about these lizards until 1910. That is when some visitors to the island first saw them. Today, Komodo dragons are **rare.** There are only about four thousand still alive. In the wild, they all live on Komodo and a few islands close to it.

Would you like to see these lizards? You do not have to make the long **journey** to Indonesia. You can see them at several zoos around the country, including the national zoo in Washington, D.C. However, do not look for them at your **local** petting zoo. Do you know why?

Answer each of the questions with a sentence.

1 Why would it be **rare** to see a Komodo dragon in this country?

_____

_____

2 How did people outside Komodo first become **aware** of Komodo dragons?

_____

_____

3 Why is a **journey** to Komodo impossible by car?

_____

_____

4 What kind of help could **local** people give you if you wanted to travel across Komodo Island?

_____

_____

5 How does a Komodo dragon use its **fangs?**

_____

_____

atlas
aware
boar
equator
fang
fierce
hoof
journey
local
rare

6 How might a deer use its **hooves** to defend itself against the dragon?

_____

_____

7 Which do you think a Komodo dragon would prefer for a meal—a wild **boar,** a deer, or a snake? Explain your answer.

_____

_____

8 Which details in the passage show that the Komodo dragon is **fierce?**

_____

_____

9 Where would you look in an **atlas** to find Washington, D.C.?

_____

_____

10 How do the lengths of days and nights compare on Komodo because it is fairly close to the **equator?**

_____

_____

Fun FACT

- Words that sound the same but have different spellings and different meanings are called homophones. **Boar** and **bore** are an example. A boar is a wild pig. To bore people is to make them lose interest. Most of us would not be **bored** if a **boar** were running toward us!

© SSI · DO NOT DUPLICATE

aware

adjective Knowing of or about something.

Word Family

awareness (noun)
un**aware** (adjective)

Context Clues

These sentences give clues to the meaning of **aware**.

> Micah was **aware** that his shirt was too big for him.

> Kim was **aware** of the rain because she could hear it hitting the roof.

> Were you **aware** that there is a party tomorrow?

Discussion & Writing Prompt

If you are standing behind someone, how can you make that person **aware** of you?

2 min.	3 min.
1. Turn and talk to your partner or group.	**2.** Write 1–3 sentences.
Use this space to take notes or draw your ideas.	Be ready to share what you have written.

Lesson 11

Review

Crossword Puzzle Solve the puzzle by writing the missing word in each sentence in the boxes with the matching numbers. The number after each clue is the lesson the word is from.

ACROSS

2. My horse limped because of the stone in its _____. (11)

5. The wild _____ ran into the forest. (11)

6. Countries near the _____ often have warm weather. (11)

9. Pigeons are not _____ birds. (11)

10. The country just north of the United States is _____.

12. There are eleven players on a soccer _____.

13. The _____ of this tiger are two inches long. (11)

DOWN

1. Our _____ across the country took about a week by car. (11)

3. The great white shark is a _____ hunter. (11)

4. Our _____ radio station listed all the schools that closed. (11)

7. I was not _____ that I had the wrong bag until I opened it. (11)

8. Red and yellow make _____.

11. If you look in the _____, you can find the location of Mali. (11)

© SSI • DO NOT DUPLICATE

Study the words. Then do the exercises that follow.

arch

n. A curved piece of wood, stone, or metal over an open space. It supports the weight above it.

We walked beneath the stone **arch** to enter the small garden.

attention

n. Thinking, listening, or watching carefully.

Nothing could draw Tan's **attention** away from the mystery he was reading.

 Show your partner how you pay attention to what she or he says.

award

n. Something given for doing well.

Shelley thanked the judges for the dictionary, her **award** for winning the state spelling contest.

v. To give something as a prize or a reward.

The judges **awarded** our dog Morgan the first prize for how well he obeyed commands.

 Tell your partner about an award you want to win.

collapse

v. 1. To fall down suddenly or to cave in.

My brothers and I built a tent from tree branches and an old blanket, but it **collapsed** when we all tried to crawl inside.

2. To fold together.

These chairs **collapse** so they are easy to store in the closet.

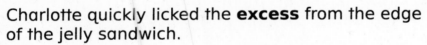

Show your partner how you pretend to collapse.

demolish

v. To destroy or tear something down.

The hurricane **demolished** a dozen houses close to the beach.

excess

adj. more than is needed or allowed.

Dad had to pay extra for his plane ticket because he had **excess** baggage.

n. An amount that is too much or more than is needed.

Charlotte quickly licked the **excess** from the edge of the jelly sandwich.

Act like you have excess books in your arms to give to your partner.

© SSI • DO NOT DUPLICATE

outline

n. 1. A line showing the outside edge of an object or figure.

Gary drew an **outline** of Asia, and then he filled in the different countries.

2. A short list or plan that gives the main ideas of a longer report.

Our **outline** will show you what we want to do for our report on turtles.

Discuss with your partner an outline for how to clean your room.

sculpture

n. A work of art made by shaping wood, stone, or other material into a certain form.

The **sculpture** of the knight on a horse stood near the entrance to the museum.

spade

n. A tool for digging. It often has a long handle fastened to a flat metal blade.

Using a **spade,** Omar helped his mom dig holes to plant seeds in the garden.

utensil

n. A tool or container that is used for a special purpose.

Esperanza put the can opener in a drawer with the other kitchen **utensils.**

12A

Completing Sentences

Circle each answer choice that correctly completes the sentence. Each question has three correct answers.

1 A **utensil** might be used for
(a) opening cans.
(b) scrambling eggs.
(c) flipping hamburgers.
(d) watching television.

2 An **excess**
(a) is a machine that runs by itself.
(b) of visitors caused the room to be too crowded.
(c) is the opposite of not enough.
(d) of water results in flooding.

3 To **collapse** is to
(a) fold for easy storage.
(b) drop to the ground suddenly.
(c) fall down because there is no support.
(d) give money or another form of help.

4 An **award**
(a) is an act that is against the law.
(b) can be in the form of a medal.
(c) is given for good behavior.
(d) can be put on display.

5 An **outline**
(a) is a list of websites for our project.
(b) is a complete report.
(c) is a line showing the outside edge.
(d) is a short plan giving the main idea.

© SSI • DO NOT DUPLICATE

Making Connections

Circle the letter next to the correct answer.

4 Which word goes with *destroy?*
(a) demolish   (b) invent   (c) outline   (d) rotate

4 Which word goes with *curved?*
(a) rare   (b) arch   (c) award   (d) journey

4 Which word goes with *dig?*
(a) net   (b) hive   (c) sculpture   (d) spade

4 Which word goes with *art?*
(a) attention   (b) astronomy   (c) sculpture   (d) equator

4 Which word goes with *listening?*
(a) invention   (b) attention   (c) demolition   (d) rotation

arch
attention
award
collapse
demolish
excess
outline
sculpture
spade
utensil

12C

Using Context Clues

Circle the letter next to the word that correctly completes the sentence.

① The prize was _____ to the winner.
   (a) collapsed   (b) demolished   (c) reflected   (d) awarded

② Stop talking, Pim! The coach really needs your _____.
   (a) award   (b) outline   (c) attention   (d) alarm

③ Draw a(n) _____ of a star for my little sister.
   (a) sculpture   (b) outline   (c) story   (d) cube

④ The _____ food was put away to eat later.
   (a) balance   (b) degree   (c) excess   (d) outline

⑤ A can opener is a very useful _____.
   (a) award   (b) scoop   (c) girder   (d) utensil

12D

Vocabulary in Context

Read the passage.

Castles of Sand

Do you enjoy building sandcastles? Then you might like to explore Jetties Beach. The beach can be found on Nantucket, an island of Massachusetts.

• • • • • • • • • • • •

The time to visit is on the second or third Saturday in August. That is when the beach holds Sandcastle and **Sculpture** Day. It is one of the most popular summer events on the island. The judges give **awards** for the best result in four different contests. There is one contest for families. There

© SSI • DO NOT DUPLICATE

is one for children under ten, too. In fact, there are contests for people of all ages. Everyone gets a chance to take part.

The first step is to sign up. The second is to know the best way to build with sand. You need to make something that will draw the judges' **attention.** To win the top prize, you need the right tools. You should have plastic **utensils.** A large bucket, a **spade,** a knife, and some spoons are a good start. Besides these, bring some paper cups of different sizes. You should also have a straw. Use it to blow away **excess** sand.

Be careful to build your sandcastle in the right place. It should be close to the water's edge. The sand there is wet. It will hold its shape. You do not want to be too close to the water, however. A big wave might come. It could **demolish** your form.

Begin by drawing an **outline** of your castle with a stick. Next, dump sand in the middle of the space. Pour water over it. Let the water drain away. Then pack the sand tightly on all sides. You can use a brick to do this. A piece of wood would work, too. Keep doing this until the pile of sand is the height you want.

Cut away sand on four sides to make your castle take shape. Try to keep the sides in balance. If you cut away sand on one side, be sure to do the same on the other. This way your castle will not **collapse** under its own weight. Your sides and top should be flat. Then you can work on the towers for each corner. Fill a paper cup with wet sand. Make sure to press it in firmly. Find the spot where you want to put the tower. Then flip the cup over quickly. You want the sand to come out in one piece. You do not want it falling apart. Do this very carefully for each tower.

You can make four walls running along the top of your castle to join the towers. Lay down lines of wet sand. Shape them with a plastic knife. Make windows and doors in the walls. You can do this by scooping out sand with a plastic

| arch |
| attention |
| award |
| collapse |
| demolish |
| excess |
| outline |
| sculpture |
| spade |
| utensil |

spoon. You could shape each of these like an **arch.** This will make the castle look like those of long ago. Finish your building by decorating it. You can use little flags, seashells, pebbles, and seaweed.

Of course, you do not have to make a sandcastle. You can build anything you like. You might try making a cat. Or what about an automobile? You could also make an octopus, a rocket ship, or a flying saucer. When you are finished, look at what other people have made. You may not win the contest. But you will still have lots of fun.

Answer each of the questions with a sentence.

1 Why is a **spade** a useful tool to have when building sandcastles?

_____

_____

2 Why is it a good idea to make an **outline** of your sandcastle?

_____

_____

3 What are some **utensils** you would use to build a sandcastle?

_____

_____

4 What is a good way to make an **arch** out of sand?

_____

_____

5 Why must you pay **attention** to where you build your sandcastle?

_____

_____

© SSI • DO NOT DUPLICATE

6 What are some other ideas for sand **sculptures** besides the ones listed in the passage?

_____

_____

7 Why do you think it is hard to build something if there is an **excess** of water in the sand?

_____

_____

8 Why might your sandcastle **collapse** before it is finished?

_____

_____

9 When might you want to **demolish** your sandcastle?

_____

_____

10 If you were a judge, how would you decide which work to choose for an **award**?

_____

_____

arch
attention
award
collapse
demolish
excess
outline
sculpture
spade
utensil

Fun
FACT

• •

• One thing that has an **arch** shape is a bow for shooting arrows. That's why the skill of shooting arrows is called archery.

outline

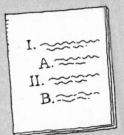

noun A short list or plan that gives the main ideas of a longer report.

noun A line showing the outside edge of an object or figure.

Academic Context

An **outline** is a plan for writing. If you want to write a story, you can first list the things that will happen and then write your story.

Discussion & Writing Prompt

If you were going to write a story about your day today, what would you put in your **outline?**

2 min.	3 min.
1. Turn and talk to your partner or group.	**2.** Write 1–3 sentences.
Use this space to take notes or draw your ideas.	Be ready to share what you have written.

© SSI • DO NOT DUPLICATE

Lesson 12

Review

Hidden Message Write the word that is missing from each sentence in the boxes next to it. The number after a sentence is the lesson the word is from. The shaded boxes will answer this riddle:

What can go around the world while staying in its own corner?

1. We walked under an _____ to enter the library. (12)

2. Bring a _____ to loosen the dirt. (12)

3. The heavy snow caused the roof to _____. (12)

4. You can remove the _____ fat with this spoon. (12)

5. Please pay _____ to me. (12)

6. The police officer gave a sharp _____ on his whistle to stop the traffic. (9)

7. I began by drawing a circle with a _____ of three inches. (10)

8. My cooking _____ are in there. (12)

9. Ellie drew an _____ of a fox and then filled in the details. (12)

10. I received an _____ for my science project. (12)

11. Strong winds could _____ our tree house. (12)

12. A wooden _____ of a bear stood near the door. (12)

Study the words. Then do the exercises that follow.

bustle

n. Busy and noisy movement.

Felix and Delia waited in the **bustle** of the lobby for the doors of the theater to open.

v. To move around in a busy, excited way.

The students **bustled** from table to table choosing materials to make masks.

channel

n. 1. The bed or path of a river or stream.

The **channel** of this river is not deep enough for these large boats.

2. A groove or cut that allows water to pass through it.

Mr. Skura built a brick **channel** down the slope to drain excess water from the garden.

3. A body of water joining two larger bodies of water.

The English **Channel** joins the North Sea and the Atlantic Ocean.

4. A way to carry an electrical signal to a television set.

Without cable, our television doesn't get very many **channels.**

Tell your partner how you would build a channel in the sand.

© SSI • DO NOT DUPLICATE

connect

v. To join or bring together.

Follow Sea Street until it **connects** to the main highway.

 Show your partner how you connect your hands.

empire

n. A number of countries or areas under the control of a single ruler or government.

For several hundred years, the Romans ruled an **empire** that included all the countries around the Mediterranean Sea.

mention

v. To speak of something without going into a lot of detail.

Did Carlos **mention** to you that he would be at the swimming pool this afternoon?

peak

n. 1. The pointed top of a mountain.

The highest **peak** in Africa is Mount Kilimanjaro.

2. Any pointed top.

Vera whipped the cream into stiff **peaks.**

 Show your partner with your hands how an ice-cream cone comes to a peak.

scholar

n. A person who has studied a subject and knows a great deal about it.

The **scholar** who wrote this book describes the houses and food of the Iroquois people living in the 1700s.

settle

v. 1. To come to rest.

A thick fog **settled** over the trees and houses, leaving only gray shadowy forms.

2. To decide about some problem.

Mrs. Reyes **settled** the argument between Diane and me by having us find the answer in the dictionary.

3. To live in a place and make it one's home.

When Sheng came to the United States from Laos, she **settled** in Houston, Texas.

Talk to your partner to settle who will go first next time.

vehicle

n. Anything on wheels or runners used to carry people or things from place to place.

An emergency **vehicle** raced along the crowded street with its sirens wailing.

Tell your partner the names of different kinds of vehicles.

zigzag

n. A line that angles as it changes direction from side to side.

The skier made a **zigzag** down the side of the hill.

v. To change direction at an angle by moving from side to side.

Matt and Ana carefully **zigzagged** the canoe past several rocks in the river.

© SSI • DO NOT DUPLICATE

13A

Words and Their Meanings

Look at the group of words next to the number. Then circle the letter next to the word that has the same meaning.

1 a line that moves at an angle from side to side
(a) channel   (b) zigzag   (c) peak   (d) vehicle

2 a cut to let water pass
(a) bustle   (b) empire   (c) channel   (d) scholar

3 to make a place one's home
(a) settle   (b) mention   (c) bustle   (d) connect

4 many countries controlled by one ruler
(a) peak   (b) vehicle   (c) scholar   (d) empire

5 a person who knows many things about a subject
(a) peak   (b) scholar   (c) vehicle   (d) bustle

Look at the word next to the number. Then circle the letter next to the group of words that has the same meaning.

bustle
channel
connect
empire
mention
peak
scholar
settle
vehicle
zigzag

6 vehicle
(a) a wild animal with fangs   (b) an object that makes things look closer
(c) something to carry people or things   (d) a curved piece over an open space

7 mention
(a) say something about   (b) look at something for a time
(c) keep a secret   (d) move to a different place to live

8 connect

(a) come to rest　　　　　　(b) take apart

(c) move quickly　　　　　　(d) join things

9 bustle

(a) noisy actions　　　　　　(b) silence

(c) top of a mountain　　　　(d) quiet music

10 peak

(a) a deep hole　　　　　　(b) a pointed top

(c) a small opening　　　　　(d) a tool for digging

13B Seeing Connections

Look at each group of words. Three are related in some way. Find the one word that does not belong and circle it.

1 sea　　　channel　　　lake　　　mountain

2 bat　　　ball　　　empire　　　glove

3 settle　　　go　　　depart　　　leave

4 say　　　listen　　　tell　　　mention

5 cut　　　chop　　　break　　　connect

© SSI • DO NOT DUPLICATE

13C

Applying Meanings

Circle the letter next to the correct answer.

1 Where will you not see much **bustle?**
(a) on an empty train (b) at a street festival
(c) at a crowded airport (d) at noon in the cafeteria

2 Which of the following is a **vehicle?**
(a) a slide (b) a slope
(c) a sled (d) a swing

3 Which of the following is a **peak?**
(a) a crater (b) a snowflake
(c) a tall building (d) a mountain top

4 Which word best describes a **zigzag?**
(a) yellow (b) angled
(c) straight (d) salty

5 Where might **scholars** do a lot of work?
(a) in a swimming pool (b) on a hike
(c) in a library (d) in their sleep

bustle
channel
connect
empire
mention
peak
scholar
settle
vehicle
zigzag

13D Vocabulary in Context
Read the passage.

The Lost City of the Incas

Do you think a city can just disappear? That is what people believed about Machu Picchu, Peru. This city was hidden from view for nearly four hundred years. It was finally found in 1911. Let's explore it!

• • • • • • • • • • •

Peru, a country in South America, has some of the highest mountains in the world. They are part of the Andes mountain chain. These mountains run along the western coast of South America. Some **peaks** are over 22,000 feet high. Travel in this area is not easy. Some places are almost impossible to reach. However, long ago, people did **settle** in these parts. They are known to us as the Incas. Machu Picchu was one of the many cities that they built.

This city is high in the Andes. There are steep cliffs on all sides. Some are 2,000 feet high. All the buildings are made from large blocks of stone. These were carefully cut to fit together exactly. How were they able to move such big stones into place? Not even **scholars** know. The Incas never invented a wheel. The Andes paths are too steep. **Vehicles** with wheels would have been useless. The city streets **connect** to each other by steps. These lead from one level to the next. Most of the buildings are one-room houses. They were built around open spaces. **Channels** were cut into the stone. They carried water into the homes.

We know very little about the people of Machu Picchu. The Incas did not leave any records. They never invented a way to write. We do know, however, that they were artistic. Faces and strange animal shapes are carved in the stones around the city. They were also skilled astronomers. They studied the stars to learn when seasons would begin and end.

© SSI • DO NOT DUPLICATE

They showed the seasons by marks carved in the stone. Their clocks were made of stone, too. They measured time as the shadow of the sun passed across their faces.

In 1532, a small Spanish army arrived. They overcame the Incas. They took control of their cities. Peru became part of Spain's **empire.** No one knows what happened to the people of Machu Picchu. The Spanish never **mention** the city in any of their records. Time passed. Some people believed an old city lay hidden in the mountains. Almost four hundred years later, explorers found it. It was covered over by trees and bushes.

These plants were cut back. The city stood as it once had. Today, many people visit it. Most fly to Cuzco, a city in southern Peru. About a half million people live there. Visitors then take a four-hour train ride up the mountain. The last part of the journey by bus can be scary. Nervous people are told not to look out of the windows. This is because the bus slowly **zigzags** its way up a road. This road is cut into the steep side of the mountain.

The trip to the top lasts about twenty minutes. Once there, visitors can enjoy the wonderful views of the Andes in all directions. They are free to explore the city. They can think about the people who built it. The streets of Machu Picchu were silent for almost four hundred years. Today, they are once again filled with the **bustle** of people.

bustle
channel
connect
empire
mention
peak
scholar
settle
vehicle
zigzag

Answer each of the questions with a sentence.

1. When did the Spanish begin to **settle** in Peru?

_____

_____

2. Why would you expect a lot of **bustle** in the center of Cuzco?

_____

_____

3 How are Cuzco and Machu Picchu **connected?**

_____

_____

4 Do you think you would be nervous on the road that **zigzags** up to Machu Picchu? Explain your answer.

_____

_____

5 What is special about the view from a mountain **peak?**

_____

_____

6 Why would the **channels** have been very important to the people of Machu Picchu?

_____

_____

7 Why didn't the Incas ever use **vehicles** with wheels?

_____

_____

8 Name a country in South America that became part of the Spanish **empire.**

_____

_____

9 Why do you think the Spanish did not **mention** Machu Picchu in their records?

_____

_____

© SSI • DO NOT DUPLICATE

10 What do **scholars** know about the people of Machu Picchu?

_____

_____

Fun FACT

- **Peak** and **peek** are an example of a homophone pair. To peek is to look at something quickly or secretly.

  *Andres **peeked** into the room to see if the baby was still sleeping.*

| bustle |
| channel |
| connect |
| empire |
| mention |
| peak |
| scholar |
| settle |
| vehicle |
| zigzag |

13 Vocabulary Extension

channel

noun A path, made by humans, that lets water pass through.

noun An area of water that connects two larger areas of water.

· ·

Other Meanings

noun A way to carry an electrical signal to a television set.

noun A way you send information, such as communication or electricity.

Discussion & Writing Prompt

If you saw a puddle, how would you make a **channel** for water to flow from that puddle to another place?

2 min.	**3 min.**
1. Turn and talk to your partner or group.	**2.** Write 1–3 sentences.
Use this space to take notes or draw your ideas.	Be ready to share what you have written.

© SSI • DO NOT DUPLICATE

Lesson 13 Review

Crossword Puzzle Solve the puzzle by writing the missing word in each sentence in the boxes with the matching numbers. The number after each clue is the lesson the word is from.

ACROSS

2. Five _____ are parked on the street. (13)

5. The _____ of the roof is forty feet above the ground. (13)

10. Does this road _____ to the main highway? (13)

11. The _____ on these pants are too long.

12. After several visits there, my aunt decided to _____ in Iowa. (13)

13. We often drink a glass of _____ juice with breakfast.

DOWN

1. Seven days make one _____.

3. Which is the all-news television _____? (13)

4. The _____ at the station died down once the train left. (13)

6. Many countries in South America were once part of the Spanish _____. (13)

7. A French _____ wrote this history of Paris. (13)

8. Did your cousin _____ that she won the race? (13)

9. My shirt has a _____ design. (13)

Study the words. Then do the exercises that follow.

adult

n. A person, animal, or plant that is fully grown.

After the picnic, the **adults** sat at the table talking, while the children played in the yard.

adj. Fully grown.

An **adult** giraffe stands eighteen feet tall, making it the tallest animal on Earth.

Tell your partner one difference between an adult dog and a puppy.

clump

n. A group of things that grow close to each other or are packed tightly together.

Beyond the **clump** of trees near the road, Sara could see the lake.

v. To walk in a way that makes a heavy, dull sound.

Jalen **clumped** into the changing room, sat on a bench, and took off his ice skates.

curious

adj. 1. Eager to learn about people or things.

Finding a tiny nest in the weeds, Pierre was **curious** to know what bird had made it.

2. Strange or unusual.

In a dusty corner of the attic, Elena found a small box with a **curious** shiny stone inside.

Discuss with your partner a curious thing about your school.

© SSI • DO NOT DUPLICATE

gratitude

n. A feeling of thanks for a gift, a favor, or some other kindness.

We sent a thank-you note to our neighbors to show our **gratitude** for their help while Mom was in the hospital.

Talk to your partner about someone you feel gratitude toward.

herd

n. A group of animals that live or move about together.

The two dogs drove the **herd** of cows through the gate and into the farmyard.

newcomer

n. Someone who has just arrived in a place.

Mr. Barton welcomed the two **newcomers** from Canada to our class.

plain

adj. 1. Simple, not fancy.

Deirdre wanted to build a **plain** birdhouse, but Maya wanted one with an opening in the shape of an arch.

2. Easy to see or understand.

The happy smile on Rosario's face made it **plain** that she was pleased to see her cousin.

n. A large piece of flat land with few trees.

Tall grasses covered the **plain** for as far as we could see.

Point to one plain thing and one fancy thing in the classroom.

stalk

n. The main stem of a plant.

Ricardo checked the **stalks** of corn for any ears that might be ripe.

v. 1. To walk in a stiff way that shows one is hurt or angry.

Even though his brother said he was sorry, Craig **stalked** out of the room with his broken airplane.

2. To follow something in a quiet way in order not to be seen.

The cheetah **stalked** the antelope carefully for several minutes, waiting for the best time to begin the chase.

Show your partner how you would stalk out of a room if you were angry.

tusk

n. A long, curved, very large tooth that sticks out of the mouths of animals like elephants or walruses.

The walrus uses its **tusks** to dig in the bottom of the sea for clams.

wealthy

adj. Having a great amount of money, property, or valuable things.

The iron and coal in the ground made England a very **wealthy** country.

© SSI • DO NOT DUPLICATE

14A

Completing Sentences

Circle each answer choice that correctly completes the sentence. Each question has three correct answers.

1 A **stalk**

(a) is the long curved tooth of an elephant.

(b) bends in the wind.

(c) is the main stem of a plant.

(d) supports the leaves of a plant.

2 A **herd** of

(a) elephants gathered at the waterhole.

(b) dust covered the shelves.

(c) cows kept us supplied with milk.

(d) deer ate grass together in a field.

3 To be **curious** is to

(a) want to learn more.

(b) be strange in some way.

(c) be in serious trouble.

(d) ask lots of questions.

4 To **clump** is to

(a) grow together bunched up.

(b) walk with heavy footsteps.

(c) be packed close together.

(d) move to higher ground.

5 Something that is **plain** is

(a) cooked rather than raw.

(b) easy to understand.

(c) without decoration.

(d) not fancy.

adult
clump
curious
gratitude
herd
newcomer
plain
stalk
tusk
wealthy

14B

Making Connections

Circle the letter next to the correct answer.

1 Which word goes with *tooth?*
(a) spade   (b) clump   (c) tusk   (d) stalk

2 Which word goes with *money?*
(a) wealthy   (b) curious   (c) plain   (d) tangled

3 Which word goes with *land?*
(a) newcomer   (b) plain   (c) adult   (d) tusk

4 Which word goes with *grown?*
(a) adult   (b) degree   (c) newcomer   (d) scholar

5 Which word goes with *thanks?*
(a) caution   (b) display   (c) curiosity   (d) gratitude

14C

Using Context Clues

Circle the letter next to the word that correctly completes the sentence.

1 The grass grows in _____.
(a) herds   (b) clumps   (c) tusks   (d) peaks

2 Miguel keeps a _____ of cows on his farm.
(a) herd   (b) stalk   (c) display   (d) fold

3 Laila watched her cat _____ the mouse.
(a) herd   (b) construct   (c) absorb   (d) stalk

© SSI • DO NOT DUPLICATE

4 Show your _____ by thanking her.

   (a) muscle   (b) wealth   (c) gratitude   (d) curiosity

5 The _____ hoped he might make lots of friends.

   (a) newcomer   (b) herd   (c) couple   (d) sapling

14D   Vocabulary in Context
Read the passage.

Elephant Country

An African elephant is huge. It is the biggest of all land animals. It is also the most powerful. But when it is very young, it is just like any other baby. It is helpless. Without its mother, a baby elephant in the wild will probably die. Not if it's cared for by Daphne Sheldrick, though. Let us explore Kenya. Let's learn about this woman and the baby elephants she saves.

• • • • • • • • • • •

Kenya is in East Africa. There the great African **plain** stretches across much of the country. Tall grass grows everywhere. **Clumps** of trees are spread here and there. All kinds of animals live in this wild place. There are elephants, of course. There are also giraffes, rhinos, and hippos. **Herds** of gazelles, impalas, and zebras are there, too. These animal herds move from place to place, looking for food. At a distance, lions **stalk** the herds. So do leopards.

Kenya has several national parks. On these lands, people are not allowed to hunt. These parks are very large. They can cover thousands of square miles. Kenya cannot hire enough park rangers to protect all of the animals, though. It is not

adult
clump
curious
gratitude
herd
newcomer
plain
stalk
tusk
wealthy

wealthy enough. People continue to hunt elephants. They want their valuable ivory **tusks.** Ivory looks like bone. It can be carved into objects. These objects sell for great amounts of money.

Some of the **adult** elephants killed are mothers. These mothers often have young babies. Some are too young. The baby elephants may be just a few days old. They are often sick and hungry. Rangers could do nothing for them. Then in 1977, things changed. Daphne Sheldrick began to care for the baby elephants.

Daphne grew up in Kenya. She lives in a house in one of the smaller national parks. The park rangers bring her the baby elephants. These babies have no mothers. She, her daughter Jill, and several trained workers feed the babies. They feed them by bottle until they are ready for solid food. They also care for them. The babies must be watched over night and day.

When they are about two years old, the young elephants are taken to Tsavo National Park. This is one of Kenya's biggest parks. For the first few weeks, the young elephants stay inside a fenced area. This helps them become familiar with their new home. All elephants are **curious.** Elephants already living in Tsavo may come look at the newcomers. The **newcomers** and these older elephants soon become comfortable with each other. That's when the young ones can leave the fenced area.

Daphne Sheldrick knows that the older elephants will look after the young ones. Sometimes she and Jill visit Tsavo National Park. When they do, many of the elephants they once cared for come up to them. They wrap their trunks around Daphne and Jill. They squeeze them gently. Daphne believes that they are showing their **gratitude.** She says that is a wonderful reward. It is the only one that she, her daughter, and their many helpers look for.

© SSI • DO NOT DUPLICATE

Answer each of the questions with a sentence.

1 How do you think an elephant uses its **tusks?**

_____

_____

2 Why is the African **plain** such a good place for animals to live?

_____

_____

3 In what way is Kenya a **wealthy** country?

_____

_____

4 What kinds of animals do you think live in the **clumps** of trees on the African plain?

_____

_____

5 Why do you think people still **stalk** elephants even when it is not allowed?

_____

_____

6 Why might it be easy for hunters to find a **herd** of elephants?

_____

_____

7 How does Daphne Sheldrick think the elephants show their **gratitude** to her and her workers?

_____

_____

adult
clump
curious
gratitude
herd
newcomer
plain
stalk
tusk
wealthy

8 What care does Sheldrick give to the baby elephants that are **newcomers** to her place?

_____

_____

9 How do the **adult** elephants help the young ones that are returned to Tsavo National Park?

_____

_____

10 Which animals in the passage are you **curious** to know more about?

_____

_____

Fun FACT

· ·

- **Herd** and **heard** are another example of a homophone pair. _Heard_ is the past tense of _hear._

  The noise I **heard** _outside my window sounded like a_ **herd** _of buffalo running down the street._

© SSI • DO NOT DUPLICATE

14 Vocabulary Extension

adult

adjective A fully grown human or animal.

. . . .

Academic Context

When an animal is born, it is a baby. An **adult** animal is grown up.

Synonyms and Antonyms

Synonyms: grown up, mature

Antonyms: baby, young

Discussion & Writing Prompt

Explain how an **adult** chicken is different from a baby chick.

2 min.	3 min.
1. Turn and talk to your partner or group.	2. Write 1–3 sentences.
Use this space to take notes or draw your ideas.	Be ready to share what you have written.

Lesson 14 Review

Hidden Message Write the word that is missing from each sentence in the boxes next to it. The number after each sentence is the lesson the word is from. The shaded boxes will answer this riddle:

The more of these you make, the more you leave behind. What are they?

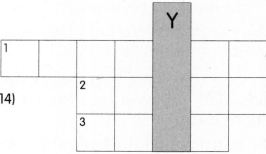

1. We saw a very _____ fish at the aquarium. (14)

2. The _____ swan watched over her babies. (14)

3. The dog chased the stray sheep back to the _____. (14)

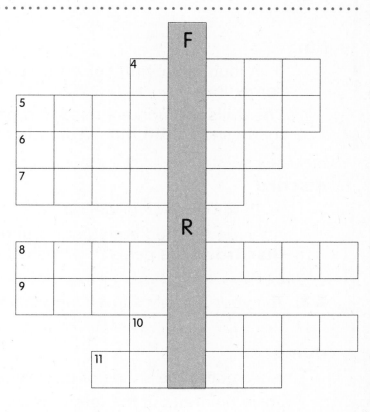

4. In the summer, we often buy corn from our _____ farmers. (11)

5. We welcomed the _____ to our club. (14)

6. My family is not _____, but we have everything we need. (14)

7. The planets formed from _____ of dust and gas. (14)

8. We showed our _____ for their help by inviting them to dinner. (14)

9. The cake was very _____ without any frosting. (14)

10. The heavy rain bent many flower _____ to the ground. (14)

11. Your drawing of the elephant shows its long _____ very well. (14)

© SSI • DO NOT DUPLICATE

Study the words. Then do the exercises that follow.

base

n. 1. The lowest part of something.

The **base** of the Washington Monument is just over fifty-five feet wide.

2. A place where the people in the army, navy, or air force do their work.

Tom's father is training for the air force at a **base** in San Antonio, Texas.

3. One of the four corners of the infield in baseball. A player must touch each one to score a run.

After Tracey hit the ball, she raced to first **base**.

 Show your partner the base of your chair or desk.

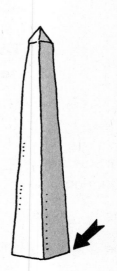

din

n. A loud, annoying noise that continues for some time.

The drills the workers used to repair the street made such a **din** that we had to close the windows.

discard

v. To throw away or get rid of.

After we finished eating our oranges, Eva **discarded** the peels in a trash can.

 Tell your partner something you discard every day.

dome

n. A roof in the shape of an upside-down bowl.

Josie pointed out the large golden **dome** of the state house as we drove into the city.

gallon

n. A measure for liquids. It equals four quarts.

For the school May Breakfast, our class made two **gallons** of orange juice.

instrument

n. 1. A tool used for doing careful work.

The dentist used one of the small **instruments** on the tray to check my teeth.

2. An object for making music.

The **instrument** that Louis Armstrong played so well was the trumpet.

luxury

n. Something that gives pleasure but is not really needed.

Dad and I had the **luxury** of front-row seats at the basketball finals.

 Tell your partner about a luxury item you want.

mallet

n. A hammer with a large head. It is made of wood or hard rubber so that it does not scratch what it hits.

Using two wooden **mallets,** Kai played a simple tune on the xylophone.

skill

n. The ability to do something well after study or training.

Reba showed great **skill** on the balance beam during our practice.

 Tell your partner about your best skill.

© SSI • DO NOT DUPLICATE

slight

adj. Small in amount or importance.

The pilot announced that there would be a **slight** delay in our landing because of the strong winds.

· ·

Show your partner how you hold your hands just a slight distance apart.

15A Words and Their Meanings

Look at the group of words next to the number. Then circle the letter next to the word that has the same meaning.

❶ something used to make music

    (a) dome   (b) gallon   (c) instrument   (d) skill

❷ four quarts

    (a) base   (b) din   (c) luxury   (d) gallon

❸ the bottom of something

    (a) skill   (b) base   (c) dome   (d) mallet

❹ a loud, continuing noise

    (a) din   (b) dome   (c) skill   (d) luxury

❺ a wooden hammer

    (a) luxury   (b) dome   (c) skill   (d) mallet

base
din
discard
dome
gallon
instrument
luxury
mallet
skill
slight

Look at the word next to the number. Then circle the letter next to the group of words that has the same meaning.

6 skill
(a) not being able to find something
(b) being able to do something well
(c) a slow way of speaking
(d) a fast way of moving

7 dome
(a) a hole in the ground shaped like a bowl
(b) a large box with a lid
(c) a high curved roof
(d) a coin with little value

8 discard
(a) get rid of
(b) look for
(c) think about
(d) run from

9 luxury
(a) a warning of danger
(b) a thing that is not needed but is enjoyable
(c) a thank-you letter
(d) a thing that causes pain

10 slight
(a) leaning to one side
(b) moving from side to side
(c) rough or uneven
(d) small in size or importance

© SSI • DO NOT DUPLICATE

15B Seeing Connections

Look at each group of words. Three are related in some way. Find the one word that does not belong and circle it.

1. mallet   golf   tennis   bowling

2. gather   collect   discard   bring

3. arch   roof   dome   herd

4. inch   gallon   yard   foot

5. slight   big   enormous   large

15C Applying Meanings

Circle the letter next to the correct answer.

base	
din	
discard	
dome	
gallon	
instrument	
luxury	
mallet	
skill	
slight	

1. Which of the following is most likely to make a **din?**
   (a) a note   (b) a butterfly   (c) a whisper   (d) a drum

2. Which of the following takes **skill?**
   (a) sleeping   (b) skating   (c) falling   (d) laughing

3. Where will you probably see an **instrument?**
   (a) in a band   (b) in a river
   (c) on a mountain   (d) on a farm

4. Which of the following is a **luxury?**
   (a) a loaf of bread   (b) a trip around the world
   (c) a glass of milk   (d) a T-shirt

5. Where would you expect to find a **base?**
   (a) on top of a car   (b) in a song
   (c) at a baseball field   (d) in a kitchen

15D Vocabulary in Context
Read the passage.

Music of the Island

Do you like music? Most of us do. When someone finds a new way to make music, people pay attention. That is what happened on a Caribbean island about seventy years ago. So let us explore Trinidad. That is where the steel drum was invented.

• • • • • • • • • • • •

Many people of Trinidad have little money for **luxuries.** Pianos and drum sets cost too much. But the people still love to make music. In the past, they sang. They kept the beat with their hands or with sticks. Then in the 1930s, they invented a new **instrument.** It was cheap and easy to make. With it, they gave the world a new sound.

Here is how it happened. The United States had a navy **base** on Trinidad. The oil for its ships came in fifty-five-**gallon** steel drums. After they were empty, the oil drums were **discarded.** These drums were great for making noise. The people of Trinidad used them in parades. The drums were played with **mallets.** They gave off one loud note when hit. Someone noticed that a dented oil drum gave two notes. One note came from the flat part; the other came from the dent. Before long, people began adding dents to the drums. That way, they could play a number of different notes. Soon they started making steel drums to keep and to sell.

Today the best steel drums are still made in Trinidad. A drum maker first cuts the oil drum all the way around. The cut is made about one foot from the top. He then uses the flat round top and the sides to make the drum. Next, he pounds the top. The maker uses a forty-pound hammer. This is called "sinking the pan." It can take up to five hours. The **din** is tremendous. He has to stretch the metal evenly without tearing it. The first steel drums had the tops pounded up from the inside. These drums had a **dome** shape. Later, people

© SSI • DO NOT DUPLICATE

decided that the sound was better if the top was pounded down from the outside. These drums have a bowl shape. Today, all steel drums are made this way.

After the top is shaped, the drum maker takes the drum to the beach. He lights a fire under it. The drum gets red hot. Then he puts it in the ocean. The drum cools quickly. This is called "tempering." It makes the metal very strong. The next step is tuning the steel drum. This is the hardest part. The drum maker strikes the pan from the inside. This makes a number of bubbles on the top. He then flattens each of them a little so that each dent gives a special note. He listens carefully to the sounds the dents make. Then he uses many small hammers to make **slight** changes. This takes great **skill.** Each note must sound clear and different from the rest. Finally, he paints the steel drum. He may also cover it in chrome. This gives the drum a bright silver finish.

Steel drums are popular all over the world. Every February, the best steel bands from many countries play in Trinidad's largest city: Port of Spain. That is when the world steel-band contest takes place. A band may have only three or four players. Or a band can have more than a hundred. The winner of the contest is most often from Trinidad. Are you surprised? Trinidad is where the steel band was born.

base
din
discard
dome
gallon
instrument
luxury
mallet
skill
slight

Answer each of the questions with a sentence.

❶ How did the navy **base** help with the invention of the steel drum?

_____

_____

❷ When would you be more likely to hear a **din**—during the steel band contest in February or during the making and tuning of the steel drums? Explain your answer.

_____

_____

3 What part of the oil drum does the drum maker probably **discard?**

_____

_____

4 Why did the drum makers change the shape of the top from a **dome** to a bowl?

_____

_____

5 How many quarts of oil are in a fifty-five-**gallon** oil drum?

_____

_____

6 How many **instruments** are in a steel-drum band?

_____

_____

7 Would a trip to Trinidad for the steel-band contest be a **luxury** for you?

_____

_____

8 How is a **mallet** used with a steel drum?

_____

_____

9 What do you think would be the best way to learn the **skill** of steel-drum making?

_____

_____

© SSI • DO NOT DUPLICATE

10 Why is it not correct to say that the drum maker heats the drum **slightly** before he puts it in the ocean?

_____

_____

FACT

• **Base** and **bass** are another example of a homophone pair. Bass is the deepest human singing voice. A bass guitar has deeper tones than a regular guitar.

Thousands of people came to hear Paul Robeson's beautiful **bass** voice.

	base
	din
	discard
	dome
	gallon
	instrument
	luxury
	mallet
	skill
	slight

skill

noun The power to do something well.

. . . .

Academic Context

In school, you practice many important **skills**, like adding, subtracting, and writing sentences with capital letters and punctuation marks.

Word Family

skilled (adjective)

skillful (adjective)

un**skill**ed (adjective)

Discussion & Writing Prompt

You may have a fun **skill**, like juggling or singing. You also have academic **skills**. Tell about a math **skill** you are learning right now.

2 min.	3 min.
1. Turn and talk to your partner or group.	**2.** Write 1–3 sentences.
Use this space to take notes or draw your ideas.	Be ready to share what you have written.

© SSI • DO NOT DUPLICATE

Review

Crossword Puzzle Solve the puzzle by writing the missing word in each sentence in the boxes with the matching numbers. The number after each clue is the lesson the word is from.

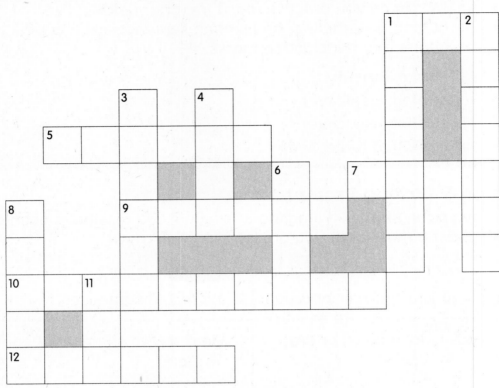

ACROSS

1. We had to shout over the _____ of the machines. (15)

5. Where is the _____ for pounding these wooden pegs into the ground? (15)

7. The _____ of this statue is at least six feet wide. (15)

9. We will need a _____ of paint for the ceiling of this room. (15)

10. Which _____ does your brother play in the band? (15)

12. For many people in the world, a car is a _____. (15)

DOWN

1. Where can I _____ these empty paint cans? (15)

2. Two _____ make a dime.

3. The kite moved even with a _____ change in the breeze. (15)

4. When the _____ rang, school began.

6. Through the glass _____, we could see blue sky. (15)

8. To have _____ at juggling takes hours of practice. (15)

11. Two plus four equals _____.

162 Review for Lesson 15